Best Young Woman Job Book

a memoir

Emma Healey

RANDOM HOUSE CANADA

Best Young Woman Job Book

a memoir

Emma Healey

RANDOM HOUSE CANADA

PUBLISHED BY RANDOM HOUSE CANADA

Published in 2022 by Random House Canada, a division of Penguin
Random House Canada Limited, Toronto. Distributed in Canada
by Penguin Random House Canada Limited, Toronto.

www.penguinrandomhouse.ca

Random House Canada and colophon are registered trademarks.

Library and Archives Canada Cataloguing in Publication

Title: Best young woman job book : a memoir / Emma Healey.
Names: Healey, Emma, 1991- author.
Identifiers: Canadiana (print) 20210257172 | Canadiana (ebook) 20210257202 |
ISBN 9780735275003 (hardcover) | ISBN 9780735275010 (EPUB)
Subjects: LCSH: Healey, Emma, 1991- | LCSH: Career changes—Canada—
Anecdotes. | LCSH: Job hunting—Canada—Anecdotes. | CSH: Authors,
Canadian (English)—Biography. | LCGFT: Autobiographies.
Classification: LCC PS8615.E253 Z46 2022 | DDC C818/.603—dc23

Text design: Lisa Jager
Jacket design: Lisa Jager

Printed in Canada

2 4 6 8 9 7 5 3 1

Penguin
Random House
RANDOM HOUSE CANADA

Then I remember more, more than I need to, about where I was living, and how I worked at my writing, driving myself relentlessly to do better and more, with moments of pleasure, but often a hounding sense of obligation, a fear that if I did not work terribly hard something would catch up with me—perhaps the possibility that I did not really need to be doing this.

—LYDIA DAVIS, "'Les Bluets,' 1973"

EVERY WEEK I GO TO THE MOVIES with Deragh and Doro, my two best friends. The Cineplex is across the street from an enormous mall in the centre of the city. To access it you have to ride three separate, steep escalators straight up. As you move into the heart of the building you pass through a constellation of globe-shaped lights, all hung from the ceiling on different lengths of wire, each glowing and dimming at its own steady pace. It is like ascending into a cloud of jellyfish inside a dream.

I like to get there early and extremely stoned, order a large popcorn with double butter, and spend a few minutes before my friends arrive contemplating the complex entanglement of art and commerce represented by the cinema. Sometimes, if they're late, I'll play ten minutes on the Metallica pinball machine hidden in the back of the small, dingy arcade near the exit. It is one of the most forgiving machines in the city.

The best part of the night is when my friends arrive and suddenly, after being apart all week, we're together. We have been doing this for years, and still, every time, when all three of us are settled in our seats amid a crowd of strangers in the dark, there's that moment when I can feel my mind slip into a lower gear.

When the movie is over we go to a bar around the corner. It occupies two floors of a large building: the ground-floor bar is moody and dark with an enormous fish tank, and the one upstairs is brightly lit and carpeted like a church basement. We pick our level based on our collective mood. Either way, when we sit close to the window we are all bathed in the cinematic red neon glow of the sign outside. They have a name for us here, like the three of us are a single person. We sing it with them, the same way, every time.

ONE

I have this photo of my parents, a few years into their relationship, sitting on the couch in my mother's apartment. The picture is over thirty years old, but nearly everything in it still exists in modified form. I pass by the apartment building almost every day on my way to work, but my mother hasn't lived in it since I was born. The beige couch they're sitting on still anchors her living room, but it's been reupholstered in deep green velvet. The couple in the photo look exactly like my mother and father, two people who are total strangers to me.

In the photo, my mother has big jeans, curly bangs and a wide grin. She's wearing an excellent sweater: cape-like, cabled red and white, draped around her shoulders. My dad, next to her, is too skinny; his glasses are cartoon '80s, and his haircut has a touch of *Eraserhead*. He looks surprised. My mother seems entirely present and uncannily comfortable, like she could reach out of the photo to grab your hand. If you merged their faces together in a computer program you would end up with exactly me.

My parents divorced when I was three, before I was old enough to really know them as a couple. When my mother first showed me this photo, several years ago when she was cleaning out her basement, I felt like I was staring at an object brought back into the real world from a dream. A postcard from an alternate timeline. I framed and hung it on my living room wall.

Not long after I did this, my dad came to visit. I hadn't thought about the fact he was going to see the picture until it was too late. When he glimpsed it he jerked back reflexively, like he'd touched an electric fence. Then he steadied himself and studied it. All of this took maybe three seconds, but it felt like a year. He stared at the picture, brow seriously furrowed, then turned to me.

This is... he said, but couldn't say what. I watched him hover for a moment above the situation, then snap back into place: *Very weird.*

His voice was taut with the tone of someone who wants plausible deniability; if you squinted, you could believe he was joking. But the picture clearly freaked him out. I wanted to ask whether it was the content of the image, or the fact that I owned and was displaying it in my house, or just the reminder that your past never belongs to you alone.

Work is one way to look at it. When my grandmother finished high school, she had the opportunity to continue her education, but her father needed her and her sister to start working full-time. She was a promising artist and an avid reader; she wanted to keep learning, but the family had rent to pay.

My grandmother worked at a few different places until she landed at an enormous publishing company. She started as a secretary and worked her way up the ladder until she became an assistant to one of the executives. Bosses loved her. She was fastidious and sensible, took perfect notes, wrote short- and longhand, never missed a detail. After work she would go to the library and check out as many books as she could carry. The money she made put my grandfather through law school. By the time my mother was born they had a son, a beautiful brick house in a nice part of town, two cars and a house in the country, a dog named Ginger and a cat named Rosie.

My grandparents took their children to plays, to concerts, to art galleries. They took road trips across the country. They travelled to New York City when my grandfather worked there, to Austria one winter for a Christmas vacation. They wanted their children's lives to feel open, full of possibility.

My mother is born with a face like a porcelain doll. She has a thousand-watt smile and rosy cheeks. She laughs at everything. For the rest of her life, the glow of her upbringing will move with her, like a spotlight.

In high school she tries smoking cigarettes so everyone will take her more seriously, but instead she just looks like an adorable twelve-year-old who smokes. At sixteen, she gets a summer job at the theatre near her parents' house in the country. She helps with the lights, drinks with the cast, flirts with the lead, feels something fuse inside her. When she tells her parents *I want to be an actor*, they say, *You can do whatever you want* and mean it.

My mother loves theatre school. She does well, makes friends, starts working right after she graduates. Local directors like her confidence, her bright eyes and fresh face. She plays a range of confident, bright-eyed, fresh-faced young women: the sister, the mistress, the secretary, second wife.

This is around when she meets my father. They have a sense of humour and a love of Bruce Springsteen in common. On their first date, he says he knows for a fact that they are going to get married and start a family. My mother rolls her eyes but agrees to see him again.

In the first half of their relationship my parents are mostly happy, with a little static. My father fears conflict so much he would rather try to climb out of their second-floor bathroom window during an argument than stay. Sometimes he shuts down completely, becomes impossible to talk to. Neither of them understands this, or any of his other unusual behaviours, as symptoms of an intense, overwhelming depression.

They get married at her parents' house in the country, hang a disco ball in the barn and invite all their friends. The party is, by all accounts, a rager. For their honeymoon, they take a road trip around America and drive home when they run out of cash. Their parents lend them money for the down payment on a house.

My parents act, my father writes, and between gigs they work. He waits tables at a very trendy restaurant inside an old movie prop warehouse, where the furniture is all mismatched antiques. As a waiter he is impressively incompetent, getting by entirely on charm. He loses Visa slips and comes home owing the restaurant money. He cannot remember any of the specials. One evening he spills a tray of red wine on an entire wedding party, soaking the bride.

My mother temps a lot, mostly answering phones in big offices. She's a good employee: efficient, cheerful, pathologically organized. Bosses love her. Sometimes they offer her money and benefits to stay on permanently, but she never says yes; she doesn't want to give up her career. One of her longest gigs is with a law firm, where she sits behind a large desk managing an elaborate network of phone lines, punching buttons with the back of a pencil and chanting the message: *Can you HOLD please? Can you HOLD please? Can you HOLD please?* Over and over. Decades later, remembering this job to me, she sings this phrase in a pitch and cadence so precise I can tell it is still burned into the circuitry of her brain. It is mesmerizing to watch. My mother is a gifted actor. By the time she's finished, I feel like it's my memory too.

When she gets pregnant, my mother tells her agent she'd like to play more *adult women*. Her agent says she'll see what she can do. The phone rings a little less.

When I'm two or three, my mother writes and stars in a one-woman show: a lightly fictionalized account of her pregnancy. Its title is the name she and my father called me before I was born; a fictional name for a real person, a true title for a play only half-based on real life.

The play is produced by a theatre festival several provinces away. It runs for a few weeks, and my mother travels out to do it. The work is strange and lonely and rewarding. Audiences are sparse but enthusiastic. It feels good to speak into the dark about her thoughts and feelings and fears. She gets a three-star review in the local paper.

A few days before the festival ends, she runs into the reviewer on the street. He tells her he actually meant to give her four stars, but the paper misprinted the piece. He suggests she photocopy his review, colour in an extra star herself, and hand it out to people on the street near the theatre. My mother does this and it works. On the last night of her run, the show is sold out. The audience gives her a standing ovation. Then she packs up her things and goes home.

When my parents divorce, my father moves into a parody of a newly single dad's apartment, a two-bedroom he shares with a man named Dan Crunt. Dan's thing is that he buys a jumbo pack of pork chops each week and separates them into seven separate Ziploc bags, each one labelled with the name of the day he plans to eat it: MONDAY, TUESDAY, WEDNESDAY, and so on.

My mother has me six days a week, more or less. She keeps the house, rents out the spare room to make the mortgage, barters with friends for childcare, sends me to my grandparents' on weekends when she can't find a sitter and in summers when she gets work out of town. She gets us a subsidized membership at the YMCA, sends me to classes so she can take a few hours for herself. Our house has two fridges—one upstairs and one down—plus a chest freezer full of home-cooked meals for babysitters to heat up. Everything is neatly labelled in her bubbly handwriting. The extra fridge is full of batteries and camera film and nail polish and bags of milk, for when we need them. The shelves in the laundry room are stacked with tomato sauce and canned beans, nails and screws in labelled drawers, spare boxes of lightbulbs and detergent. When something we need goes on sale, she buys as many of it as she can fit in the trunk of our sparkling teal Ford Escort. There are plastic bags in our home that will be washed and reused for literal decades.

My mother caters two or three or four or five nights a week, depending on the season. She usually works for the same upscale company, whose owner has come to rely on her relentless efficiency. Catering is a grinding inversion of acting, an obstacle course of setup and takedown where you're paid to perform the role of a stock image. My mother comes home after a gig, pays the babysitter a third of what she just made, maybe drinks half a glass of wine on the couch, falls dead asleep and then wakes up a few hours later to take me to school. Sometimes she packs stolen leftovers from weddings and retirement parties into my lunchbox: cucumber sandwiches cookie-cut into heart shapes, chocolate mousse cups sprinkled with gold foil.

One night, when I'm five or six years old, she's bustling around the kitchen trying to get ready before the babysitter comes. It's December, almost Christmas, the busiest season for catering work. Everything in the kitchen is tilted downward a few degrees: the yellowing linoleum, the cheerful blue walls, the chili pepper party lights strung up along the wall, the cat lazily crunching his food in the corner, the big white round table where I sit eating dinner. The foundation of our house is slowly sinking into the ground, but we don't know that yet.

This used to be a memory, but I've gone back so many times I can see it from the outside, like a scene from a film. My mother has a brutal cold, is probably too sick to be working. She fishes around in the cabinet where she keeps the vitamins and napkins, glass of water in her other hand, and comes out with a handful of cold supplements: vitamin C, echinacea, whatever. Then she walks over to the table where I'm sitting. There's a beat. My mother has excellent timing. Locking eyes with me, she crams the whole handful of pills in her mouth and throws back the glass of water after it, grimacing as she swallows. With a small flourish, she slams the glass down whiskey-shot on the table in front of me, and intones: *Sheer force of will, Emma. Sheer force of will.*

When I tell her I want to write books when I grow up, she says, *You have to do whatever makes you happy*, and she means it.

My mother does not stop acting. She does children's plays and Greek tragedies and a McDonald's commercial and video game voice-overs and a documentary play about the impacts of a hate crime in a small town and a comedy musical about people making a dramatic musical based on the movie *Top Gun* called *Top Gun! The Musical* that I can still sing through front to back with my eyes closed because of how often she plays her rehearsal cassettes in the car. In the summers, she does farces in a small-town theatre run by an old friend, playing kooky ladies in shows with titles like *Run for Your Wife* to sold-out crowds of seniors with season passes. Eventually she will meet my step-father in a show called *Wrong for Each Other*, where they play a divorced couple reminiscing about their dead relationship.

Money appears on the dining room table at unpredictable intervals. It looks like any other kind of mail. You never know where a cheque is going to come from, or how much it will be for. Sometimes a commercial you shot five years ago starts running again and you can finally pay off your credit card. Sometimes a made-for-TV movie where you played the protagonist's best friend's mother airs twice on some American channel in the middle of the night and you get sent seventeen cents. Money is abstract, governed by forces completely outside your control or understanding. It is entirely disconnected from the amount of effort you put into making it or the real value of the finished thing you made. It is asynchronous with your life, your work, your value, and also it is the only thing you really need to live.

If my mother books an audition but can't find a babysitter she'll bring me along, plonk me down in the waiting room with a book. The room is usually full of other women around her age, all there for the same part. It's a fun game to try to figure out what they have in common with each other. Often it's the colour of their skin or hair, their height, their build, their age. Each woman is always wearing the same type of clothing as all the others, pulled from their own wardrobes based on a vague description in the sides: *workout gear, business casual, slightly dishevelled,* etc. No one looks exactly the same as anyone else, but everyone looks like each other.

The chore I simultaneously dread and love the most is helping her run lines. No quiet moment in our lives together— making dinner, driving to the grocery store, half-watching something stupid on TV—is safe from her *Hey could you just help me with this for a few minutes?* I always roll my eyes, and then I say yes, and then we pass the same handful of phrases back and forth for what feels like hours.

One of the most tediously intimate things you can do with another person is to help them memorize a text. You learn the layout of their mind by seeing what sticks, which words they always want to switch out for another. It's boring, but I get a kind of satisfaction out of being good at it: knowing how long to wait before I should prompt her, whether a mistake is big enough to correct or minor enough to let slide. The whole exercise feels like a strange variation on the way we talk to each other: a private lexicon embroidered with shared references, governed by a set of rules that only we completely understand.

Usually, by the time I go to see her in a play, I know all her lines by heart. If she ever fucks up a phrase, I can feel my breath expanding in my throat, my palms sweating a little as I sit there in the dark, waiting for her to recover.

I start to notice her writing when I'm maybe eight years old. She's always written in her journal on the weekends, but she hasn't written a full play since the one about my birth. Suddenly she's bent over her notebook, scribbling and crossing things out, in almost every empty moment. While I take swimming lessons at the YMCA, she sits in the glassed-in waiting room that overlooks the pool with her notebook in her lap. Every time I come up for air I can see her, through the layers of glass that separate us; she's always staring down at the pages, completely absorbed.

One of the country's largest newspapers reserves space on the back page of the front section for personal essays, 500–800 words each, on any topic. My mother starts pitching to this section, and every few months they accept. Her essays are mostly vignettes about her life as a single mother. I only ever appear in them as a plot device, sparking action or moving it along—but still, whenever she publishes a new one, I grab the paper and scan it for mentions of me. Reading about myself gives me the same feeling I get from looking at a photo of my face, or catching it in the mirror at an unfamiliar angle: a glimpse of how I might look from the outside.

Soon, my mother starts writing plays again. She writes one about catering and one about seventeenth-century theatre and one about medically assisted death and one about a multi-generational family packing up their mother's old house before they sell it.

Almost all of these shows feature mothers and daughters. Their ages almost always track with ours. When they're younger, her daughters are curious and over-talkative—a little precocious but ultimately charming. As we get older they become dryly funny with a strong aura of calm detachment, like they're floating above the action of each scene. The mothers are like her but bad. They speak in her voice, share her sense of humour, but unlike her they are selfish and quick-tempered. They lean on their daughters too hard for companionship, treating them more like friends than children. They can be frazzled and harsh, prone to snapping. But underneath it all, you can tell they are doing their best.

When I am nine years old, each of my parents writes a play.

My father's is about three men: two farmers and one young actor who comes to study them for a role. My mother's is about three women: one in her twenties, one in her thirties and one in her forties, all going through different kinds of break-ups and heartbreak.

Both shows are first produced in small theatres, then in larger venues with bigger audiences. My mother's work is funny and relatable; my father's is moving, stirring, sad. The two plays are radically different in structure and theme, but equally well-written, emotionally impactful in their own way. People love them. They sell out.

My father's play will be picked up by a major producer, tour across the country, win multiple awards, and eventually make him enough money to singlehandedly fund six years of independent middle- and high-school education for me, plus two years of university tuition. He will be given a residency and an office at a prestigious local theatre, where there is a black-and-white photo of him hanging in the lobby. He will buy a new car and a house, then flip that house and buy another one. He will buy art from local artists, adopt a dog, take cabs when he's late to a meeting. He will never have to audition for an acting role again, or submit his writing to an editor who might reject it, if he doesn't want to.

My mother's play will also be produced across the country and around the world. It will be turned into a musical, be published in a range of different languages, run in theatres large and small for decades to come. She and her friends will even get a deal with a major publisher to write a self-help book based on its contents; they will go on the *Today* show to promote it.

She will use her third of the advance to fix the foundation of her sinking house. But she still has to audition, still submits her writing to editors who don't recognize her name, still prays for grants, takes gigs to pay the bills, resists when they invite her on full-time.

My mother's play is co-written with two of her best friends. Each woman plays a fictionalized version of herself, stalking the stage in red lipstick and a black cocktail dress. Sometimes they speak all in one voice like a Greek chorus; other times, they split apart to deliver individual monologues.

Each of the three characters has recently ended a significant relationship—with a boyfriend, a live-in partner and a husband, respectively. My mother plays an anxious, obsessive, organized single mother who's in the middle of divorcing the father of her child. The thesis of the show is that with time, even the worst parts of your life can become just a story. All you have to do is tell it again and again.

There's one scene where my mother is cleaning up her kid's toys after a long day. She's at the front of the stage on her knees next to this big blue Rubbermaid bin full of Barbie dolls. (In the show's first production they used the bin full of Barbies that normally lived untouched under my bed, all the dolls' hair fusing into a rat king–like tangle in the dark.) As she picks up Barbie and Ken, she starts acting out a scene between them.

In the beginning of their story, Barbie has a perfect life—a house, her own motorcycle, a long luxurious mane of chemical-blonde hair—and then in walks Ken, with his abs and his smooth crotch. *Oh, Ken,* she says, smothering him with kisses, *I love you so much I'm gonna work you through law school!* Ken accepts. They have a litter of doll babies, buy their dream house, are determined to move through life as a team.

But then one day he comes home from a long day at the office. *Barbie, I never loved you*, he intones. *I've decided I want to be a Mountie.* Barbie is stunned. *But Ken! What about the dream house? What about little baby Stacey? What about our life together?*

she stammers. *Nope, never loved you, want to be a Mountie,* my mother, the mother in the play, says through the doll in a low voice, gripping his legs in a tight fist.

Barbie lists off all the things she gave up to be with Ken, all the gestures he never appreciated. He just keeps repeating his mantra: *never loved you, never loved you, want to be a Mountie.* At the argument's peak, when they're screaming at each other, my mother bites Ken's head off in a fit of rage, and in a split second the joke snaps into a moment of icy silence. Now we are watching a woman in a black dress, on her knees, in a pool of light, staring at a pile of children's toys. She stays there like that, alone, for a long beat. My mother has excellent timing. Then she finishes cleaning up.

When I start high school, my mother quits catering. She has a new job, working as a Standardized Patient. SP is a program designed to help medical students practice their skills and bedside manner. Actors play sick people, and students, pretending to be doctors, diagnose them.

As an SP, my mother is always a woman between the ages of thirty-five and fifty-five. She has everything happen to her: hypertension or diabetes or a burst appendix, a difficult job or a secret drinking problem, a cold, a thyroid issue, a herniated disc, a colicky baby.

Every SP has a script: an opening line that never changes, a battery of answers to questions the doctor is most likely to ask. Every exam starts the same—*So what brings you in today?*—but my mother never just gets to tell anyone what's wrong with her. Instead, she gives little hints: her blood pressure, her other medications, how her grandfather died, how she flinches when you ask about her husband.

The scripts are structured this way to teach students that most people's ideas about themselves are basically true but practically useless. Patients do not usually give you the information you need to properly understand them. You have to ask the right questions, put the puzzle together yourself. My mother's women develop like Polaroids: disparate parts coming slowly into focus, not connected until all at once they are.

My high school is a city-block-sized building owned and operated by the city's biggest university. When it opened in the early 1900s, the school was supposed to be a pipeline, carrying academically gifted children straight into the university. But in the mid-'80s a rift opened up: the high school was no longer sending the university its best and brightest, and the university no longer wanted to pay for the building's upkeep. Unable to fully commit to or separate from each other, the two institutions stayed locked in each other's orbit, tethered by the gravity of a shared name.

By the time I get there, the building is falling apart. There is no phone or PA system connecting the classrooms. The basement is a maze of dead hallways and locked doors, some marked with signs that say ASBESTOS—KEEP OUT. The third-floor hallway is lined with enormous, ancient wooden cabinets that are sometimes locked and sometimes open; if I'm passing by and there's no one around, I'll try a few of the handles just in case. They're filled with old junk that has gone from being trash to antique: old Betamax tapes, taxidermied animals, lab beakers, unopened boxes of lightbulbs from the '60s.

Another door I like trying is the one that leads to the swimming pool. The pool is in the basement, at the base of the northeast staircase. It doesn't get used very much; often when I walk by the room, I can see through the tiny window in the door that the lights are turned off. I develop a habit of trying the doorknob absentmindedly almost every time I walk past it, and nine times out of ten it's locked. But sometimes, for some reason, it will be open, and I can step inside.

The air is always warm and damp, laced with the gently poisonous chlorine-smell of the indoor pool. Weak light from the street filters in through the wavy glass windows, throws the pattern of the water on the ceiling. All sounds from outside melt together until they're just echo. I am fascinated by this whole other world; untouched, liquid, shifting underneath the one I use each day.

I have my first-ever panic attack at age fourteen, near the end of the lunch hour on an otherwise unremarkable spring day. I am sitting out on the loading dock that overlooks the school parking lot with my boyfriend. I'm supposed to go to math class in ten minutes, but all I can think about is how I've failed to do my homework once again, how I may never understand math at all, how this fundamental flaw will hamper my growth and development in every area of my life, how it will prevent me from ever knowing true love or spiritual fulfillment, from ever getting a real job or understanding a single thing about the world, how I will die alone and penniless and unloved because of my failure. I can feel every molecule in my body vibrating. I can hear myself breathing very, very fast.

Then, somehow, I am in the principal's office. The school receptionist is sitting next to me. *This is so much more common than you think*, he says, in the kindest voice I have ever heard. Then the ground opens up under my feet.

Every once in a while the Standardized Patient program needs teens to play teen roles. Someone asks my mother if I need the money, which I do, because weed and Blink-182 CDs aren't free. Ninety percent of the girls I play are pregnant or suicidal. I rehearse a look that works plausibly for both: stooped shoulders, no eye contact, tiny tentative voice: *Are you going to tell my parents?*

Sometimes I get to work a physiotherapy exam, which is less psychically taxing but physically weirder. In these roles, I have to pretend I'm feeling a very specific kind of discomfort in a very specific part of my body, repeat the same standardized cringes and exclamations each time a student touches me there.

Depending on whether they are doing five- or ten-minute rotations, an SP can perform the same script twenty-four to forty-eight times for two twelve-hour days in a row. Strangers move in and out of the exam room, palpating the soles of my feet, sounding my liver, touching my throat, staring deeply into my eyes, the same way each time. Sometimes I close my eyes and imagine I am a statue, that the students are tourists who want to touch the same spot on my body for good luck.

By the end of my time in high school I still want to be a writer, though I'm not sure what kind. Mostly I try to write short stories, but they always end up being plotless and hard to follow—pages of allegory and metaphor so dense you can barely make out what I'm talking about.

My biggest problem is plot. I know that in fiction, things need to happen, but whenever I'm envisioning a story, I can only picture individual, crystal-clear scenes with nothing connecting them. In pessimistic moments I worry that this is an unfixable problem, one that means I will never be able to write a proper story. But when I'm feeling better about myself, I think I have the capacity to learn.

I apply to two universities: one in Canada and one in America. I know, already, that America—or New York City, which is America to me—is the place that writers go to become serious; where I could "make contacts," be discovered, sign a book deal, become real.

But I only get into the Canadian school. I try to console myself by looking at the faculty on the program's website, and it kind of works. There are poets who sound vaguely familiar to me, short story writers whose names I have seen on shelves at the bookstore. Some of them seem young and interesting. I imagine myself moving among them, wearing outfits and talking about literature.

Still, when I tell my friends or their parents or my parents' friends that I'm going to school for creative writing, I make a point of making sure they understand the scale of my ambitions. It's very important to me that everyone knows my goals are not embarrassing. *I don't want to be* famous, I say, over and over, really pressing on the word to emphasize its absurdity.

There's almost no such thing as a famous writer. I know that. *I just want to be able to make a living doing the thing I love.* I feel a little thrill every time I say this. I am impressed with myself for being so realistic.

I already have my breakthrough first novel half planned out. It's a text that will take the raw material of my life and apply a light dusting of magical realism. The protagonist will be a teen girl just a few years younger than I am. She will be brilliant, neurotic, depressed, popular for her caustic sense of humour and inherent goodness but also misunderstood, because her interior life is far too complex for anyone around her to truly grasp. The plot is a little fuzzier, but I know it revolves around a disappearance. One day her best friend doesn't come to school, stops answering her phone. When the protagonist tries to ask her friends about it, they shrug. When she tries to get in touch with the parents, they turn her away. When she asks the principal, he says the school is looking into it. Frustrated, our protagonist turns into an amateur detective, determined to find her friend.

The book takes place in a high school that is ancient and falling apart, full of mysterious dead hallways and locked doors. Somewhere in the course of her investigation, our hero discovers that one of them leads to a swimming pool that is actually a kind of black hole—an inky void into which all sound and light completely disappear.

Standing on the edge of it, she can swear she hears her best friend's voice somewhere in the darkness. But she doesn't know what to do next. She can't figure out whether the people around her know about this. She wonders why the adults in charge of the building would want to leave a functioning black hole in the basement, slowly pulling everything toward it. She wonders whether she'll be the next one to disappear.

Every time I sit down to work on the book, I try to figure out what comes after this—how our hero finds out who's responsible, and what she does about it. But for some reason I always just end up writing the same scene, again and again. She walks into the room, hears all the sounds of the building at once, a cacophony swirling and melting into the centre of the room. Feels herself being pulled into the darkness.

In my first year of university I take a fiction workshop. The professor has been working at the school for a thousand years and hates his job. He devotes most of each class to delivering long lectures on the subject of why he shouldn't have to teach us. Sometimes he gives a "prompt" that sounds like he's synopsizing the plot of an action movie, then tells us to "just write" and leaves for the evening.

The class is three hours long, with a fifteen-minute break in the middle. I sit next to a nice young man who used to play a secondary character on a popular soap opera for teens, where he was castmates with a guy who is now the most famous rapper in the entire world. During the break, he and I sprint down two flights of escalators to the student bar on the second floor. Its mascot, prominently featured on the sign above the entrance, is a winking cartoon demon, its red face faded to a pinkish, ham-like hue under the building's fluorescent lights. Inside, the windows are draped with thick blackout curtains. The air smells like bleach and stale Labatt's. It's like drinking inside a depressed person's brain. We each chug a shot and a beer as fast as we can, then run back upstairs before the break is over. This is the most valuable educational experience I have in the fiction workshop.

I take a poetry workshop too. The professor is a real writer, with published books. They wear black clothes and black-rimmed glasses and speak in a tone that is somehow both languid and sharp. I hear they used to teach in New York City. Everyone wants desperately to impress them and is terrified of their disapproval.

On our first day of class, the professor goes around the room, asking everyone to say the title of the last book of poetry they read. When my turn comes I feel hot panic stopping my throat. I stammer out the title of a book I stole off my father's nightstand eight months earlier. *At least it's contemporary*, the professor sighs. I feel chosen.

A few weeks later, when I include a prose poem in my portfolio, they return it with a note in the margins that says: *This form is yours if you want it.* I will write only prose poems for the rest of my life.

I meet people in this class: tree planters, painters, book readers, queers. I become quickly fused to the guy who sits behind me, a man named Mike who is part Labrador retriever and part dad-mystic. Mike spends his summers working on barges and speaks in the dialect of another dimension; he has a moustache like his old man and a generous laugh and a mind that sometimes spins so furiously you can see sparks in his eyes. He is quiet in class but picks up the best details in other people's writing like a magnet picking up iron filings.

Halfway through the year, we will start a literary magazine together for fun. It will last for a respectable few issues and become a time capsule of our friendship. My favourite days are the ones we spend working together in his apartment, sitting on the hardwood floor of his sparsely decorated living room with our laptops open, reading through the poetry submissions one at a time. Sometimes we don't need to speak to know that we agree. I have never had a friend this close before.

The poetry workshop has an end-of-semester reading at a local, lightless basement bar. I drink a pint of beer before my turn. When my time comes I climb up onto the stage, shifting from foot to foot, my nerves burning off in the spotlight. I read a poem I finished earlier that day while sitting at my uncomfortably tall kitchen table, frantically revising and reading out loud with an intensity that freaked out my roommate.

The poem is a kind of refracted biography. It tells the story of my birth through a lattice of small lies. It gives the general sense of the story correctly, but the details are never exactly clear—they're all scattered around and off the mark. It's about me but not me at all and I have no idea where it came from or what it means. I wrote it high on something that felt like premonition, though I know that can't be right. Like I was channelling something that already existed.

Later that night, at a house party, my friends ask me to read the poem again. I stand in front of like ten or twenty or two hundred people in a stranger's living room and read a five-minute-long poem about myself because my friends want me to and everyone is quiet, the whole way through, even though they don't have to be. People clap when I finish. I walk home weightless, changed.

At the end of the year, I enter the poem for a school prize and win a cheque for $500 and a little certificate with my name printed on it. After the ceremony I stand next to the snack table, filling up small square napkins with sweaty cheddar triangles and dry chocolate chip cookies. I'm trying to stuff as many as I can into my purse without being noticed when a man taps me on the shoulder and I jump. *Hey, I just wanted to say congratulations*, he says.

I know this man, or at least I know of him. He's a part-time teacher at the school, but more than that he's a real writer. I've seen him read at bars; I've seen his books in the display cases at the front of the department; I've seen the warm orange light spilling out of his office, which is technically the office of the literary magazine he runs out of the school, using its resources.

He tells me he was on the jury, that he wrote the citation for my work. He says he loves my poems, and that he wants to publish them in his magazine as soon as possible. He says I should send him an email. He says, *Congratulations again.*

I float home on a cloud of spun approval. The world feels open and infinite, like I could move in any direction. I can sense that I am at the beginning of something very important, a time that will determine the course of the rest of my life.

The next day I go to the bank to deposit the prize money. I use it to pay next month's rent and then it's gone, like it never existed.

TWO

Deragh is an actor and Doro is a musician. For years, they worked together at an independent movie theatre that showed only documentaries. I'd visit them at the end of their closing shift and munch on a bag of leftover popcorn while they swept the floors and turned the lights off.

Now they both work at the biggest art gallery. Doro does the coat check, while Deragh is contracted to work there for only the duration of a single incredibly popular exhibition, which has sold out so far in advance, and been extended for so long, that the gallery has hired dozens of temporary staff to run it.

The show is a retrospective look at the work of an internationally renowned sculptor and painter. Instead of individual, standalone pieces, she builds whole rooms designed to evoke a sense of intimate connection to her interior world. Viewers walk between them, feeling overwhelmed by the sensory onslaught of colour and light.

Deragh's job is to guard the most popular room, which is filled with mirrors. There are mirrors on the walls, mirrors on the floor, mirrors on the ceiling. When you stand inside the space, you're supposed to feel as though you are floating inside a space without limitation, a room that never ends.

This room is art, and it means something. It is also such a popular place to take a photo of yourself that the gallery imposes a rule: no one is allowed to spend more than twenty-five seconds inside, in order to ensure that everyone who paid for a ticket gets to experience it.

Deragh is the enforcer of this rule. For fifteen dollars an hour, she sits outside the room and instructs the next people in line not to touch anything. Once they're in, she starts a timer. After their twenty-five seconds are up, she opens the door and tells them they have to go. Sometimes she needs to escort them out. People hate being told to leave infinity.

I get a summer internship by emailing every single publisher in my hometown and saying I will do pretty much anything for experience. I can afford to make this promise because my parents pay my university tuition. One press writes back offering me a spot, as long as I don't mind splitting the honorarium with the intern they've already hired. *Of course! That's fine!* I write back immediately, hoping I sound enthusiastic enough.

My mother lets me spend the summer at home. My childhood bedroom is now a guest room, walls repainted in a tasteful shade of cream. The bed is set at a different angle against the wall, but its frame is still the same antique monstrosity I slept on for all of my young adult life, a tangle of rusted springs and metal that creaks and groans whenever I shift my weight. Every morning I wake myself up with the sound, and then lie there confused for thirty seconds as I fade back into consciousness, caught between the past and present, trying to orient myself.

This is the summer when I realize I need chemical help managing my mind. I've been having panic attacks a few times a week since that first one at the loading dock, but lately I have also been so distracted by the churn of my own thoughts that I sleep fitfully and often forget to eat meals. I find a therapist, and my doctor prescribes me pills to rebalance my brain. *Be careful with these when you're drinking*, she says as she's signing her name on the pad. *They can lower your tolerance significantly.*

The pills work. Almost immediately, something dark feels cleared off the glass. I sleep through the night, I eat three meals a day, breathe in and out and in like I'm supposed to.

The pills *do* change my tolerance for alcohol. Drinking several beers over the course of a long night, something I am used to doing multiple times a week with no consequences, now induces a throbbing hangover that makes all experience feel both sped up and lagging. I don't party that much while I'm living at home, but some weekend nights I'll retrieve a bottle of Moosehead from the downstairs fridge and drink half of it on the couch with my mother and stepfather while watching *Jeopardy!* Seven hours later, I'll wake up back in the room that's both mine and not mine with a pounding headache, shimmering nauseous in the off-white duvet. I figure I'll get used to it eventually.

The publisher's office is all the way across town. With traffic, the streetcar ride takes two hours. On the weekends I check out long, important books from the library and pack them in my courier bag. Most mornings on my way to work, I'll read one or two pages of one of these texts and then get bored and shove it back into my bag. Then I'll put on my headphones and stare out the window as the city inches past, all that literature turning to dead weight at my feet.

The publisher publishes a lot of different kinds of books. I mostly know them for their small runs of poetry and literary fiction, but once I start working there, I realize the bulk of their output is actually cookbooks, popular science, and ghostwritten celebrity biographies of teen heartthrobs. One of the editors explains to me that these books allow them to fund their more literary output, because those kinds of books don't really sell.

Everyone who works for the publisher is polite, has aggressive carpal tunnel syndrome and seems very tired. The other intern sits on the opposite end of the office; I could not tell you what she looks like or what she does all day. I'm bad at the office's phone system, too shy for small talk and afraid of the postage machine, but good at updating the website.

When they see that I can write a legible blog post, my co-workers ask if I want to learn how to edit. After some practice I'm allowed to work on a few minor titles: a collection of poetry, a musician's e-book of autobiographical short stories, a "gritty" murder mystery full of gratuitous racism and sentences so grammatically fucked up they feel like they're written in code.

I love editing. It's like being a writer but invisible, in reverse. Someone's already done all the hard work of thinking and creating, and all I have to do is remember the rules. I get a wash of jigsaw-puzzle satisfaction from taking a sentence or a paragraph apart, locating the true meaning hidden at its core, rearranging it and stitching everything back together again as neatly as possible, hiding all traces of my interference. If I do it right, you can't tell that I was ever there at all.

The publisher lets me take days off work to do Standardized Patient gigs. There's a summer training program that certain medical students need to complete in order to get their licences. It pays well and I need the money.

The summer program is designed to acclimate future doctors to some of the more uncomfortable situations they might encounter while practicing medicine. The SP roles are highly dramatic—there can be swearing, screaming, crying, gross details. *It's less of a test and more of a learning experience,* I explain to the editors over lunch. They do not care but nod politely.

The program takes place in an office building downtown instead of a hospital, like most SP jobs. The exam rooms are purpose-built, half doctor's office and half lunchroom. Each has a few rolling desk chairs, an exam table, grey carpeting and a two-way mirror so more instructors can watch from the outside. It feels like a room you might encounter in a dream—two entirely different types of familiar, generic space melted into one another.

For each exam there is an SP, a student playing their doctor, an instructor, and a small audience of other students. The fake doctor and the SP have an interaction while the rest of the class takes notes. When the class has questions, they can call a time out to ask. When the scene ends they move on to the next room, and another group of students comes in to take their place. I am still mostly pregnant or suicidal, but in more interesting, nuanced ways.

One day I'm playing the role of a young woman with heart problems. The plot of the scene is that to properly take my heartbeat, the doctor needs me to take my shirt off—but when they ask, I say I'm not comfortable. If they press, the script requires me to get panicky, defensive. I am shy and nervous. *No doctor has ever asked me to do this before*, I say. *Why can't I just keep my shirt on?* The student's job is to calmly explain that the examination works best if we do it their way. But if I keep saying no they're supposed to listen, and eventually reassure me that they'll find another way.

The day is mostly unremarkable. I do the scene four or five times with no issues. Each student is initially flustered but gets the point.

The next round starts the same as all the others. I'm sitting on the exam table in my hospital gown, legs dangling off the side. No matter how many times I do this, it still feels weird to be acting in front of an audience of fake doctors. I feel briefly vulnerable looking up at them, pencils poised against their notebooks, but I know it will stop when the timer starts. The scene always begins with the student knocking on the door, pretending to come in. This time, my doctor is a young man.

Everything starts out normally. But when I tell him I don't want to take my shirt off, he's immediately irritated. *You need to do it so I can listen to your heart*, he says. When I ask whether it's really necessary, he shakes his head, rolls his eyes. *It doesn't work if you don't take your shirt off*, he says, like he is talking to the world's dumbest baby idiot.

I'm not sure how my face looks or what I say. *Look, there's nothing to be scared of*, he says, trying and failing to conceal his impatience. That tone creeping up through his voice. Then: *You just have do it.* Then: *What don't you understand?*

He looks at his classmates for assistance. Some of them have their heads down, scribbling notes, while others stare right up at us, at him, at me. I feel a wave of something travel through me. Queasy, charged. Can he actually get me to take my shirt off? There was no guidance in the script about this. He is supposed to relent or his friends are supposed to call a time out or the instructor is supposed to step in or someone is supposed to knock on the door and tell us the time is up. But none of those things are happening. The room feels like it is getting smaller, hotter. None of the students are taking notes anymore. Everyone is staring at me.

For a second I can see this scene from the outside, like I'm looking through the two-way mirror. A man who is pretending to be a doctor is being forced into a humiliating game of pretend in front of his friends and colleagues, where he has to speak passwords into a woman pretending to be a patient until he finds the one that makes her take her shirt off, and she is making it impossible for him to succeed. *Listen*, the fake doctor says, real anger rising in his voice, *you just have to do it. It's the only way for me to do my job properly. Okay?* I try to focus on the fact that there is probably someone behind the two-way mirror. I try to remind myself that the instructor will probably not let it go much further; that there is an audience of witnesses. That this is happening *at work*, and that time will be up soon.

I can see one of his hands shaking. *Listen*, he says. *YOU JUST NEED TO DO IT.* No one calls a time out. I can feel hot tears gathering in the corners of my eyes.

Eventually it's over. I do the scene a few more times, and then I get my stuff and go back out into the world. I am paid the same for this role as I am for any other.

From my desk in the publishing office, I can hear a few of the editors on a conference call. They are talking to a writer who teaches at my university—the same one who congratulated me at the awards ceremony. He's just written a book of short stories, and they are discussing potential strategies for promoting it. The call is long. Afterwards, the editors all walk out looking irritated. *Poets*, one of the editors says, rolling his eyes. I feel a small thrill I don't completely understand.

One of my jobs as an intern is to deal with the slush pile—an enormous plastic box of unsolicited submissions that sits a few feet away from my desk. These are manuscripts people send to us without an agent or any prior relationship with the publisher, hoping that an editor will pluck their work from the pile and recognize its worth. Often the submissions begin with cover letters about how their authors have been working on them for years. The books are often about their deepest secrets, their families, their lives. I work on making a dent in the pile when I have absolutely nothing else to do. *When responding to a slush pile submission,* an editor tells me, *it's best to use phrasing that conveys, beyond a shadow of a doubt, that you never want to hear from them again.*

One afternoon, a group of people in their late twenties and early thirties appears in the office. They are tentative and gentle, slightly timid. They move through the space as quietly as they can, taking in details, murmuring. An editor tells me they're MFA students, visiting from a prestigious program designed to prepare them for the publishing industry. When the group floats up behind me, I show them my computer, the enormous plastic bin full of manuscripts I'm supposed to say no to, the phone I'm too scared to pick up. One of them says she hopes to have my job someday. The others nod.

At the end of the summer, the publisher pays me my half of the honorarium. It is about half of what I'd make in a month of minimum wage employment. I use it to buy a train ticket back to school and pay some of my September rent, and then it's gone.

On the first day of my second year of university, the poet I met at the awards ceremony invites me out to a bar with him and his friends.

They are all real writers—poets and professors and graduate students. They have chapbooks and small-press collections of poems and short stories. They are the editors of literary magazines, or at least sections of literary magazines. They move in tight packs, their own collective noun: a reading series of them, an anthology, a pending suit. They teach classes and recommend each other's books. They hold classes in bars. They go out drinking together almost every night. The more time I spend with them, the more they invite me. I accept, I accept, I accept.

There are a handful of young women in their group, but it's tough to know how many. We glimmer like a mirage, like a flock of birds in flight. Sometimes one of us disappears, only to be replaced almost immediately by another. We watch each other with suspicion, wariness, pity, jealousy, fear. We are a family, a kind of one.

The real writers are our editors, our mentors, our superiors or our peers. We take their classes or we go to a party or we come to a reading or we are just meeting a friend at the bar when they approach us. They ask what we are drinking, and then they never have to ask again.

They laugh at our jokes, arch an eyebrow when no one is looking. They think we're funny, because we are. They hold their liquor better than their friends, who pass out on and under tables, or light their cigarettes indoors, or leer and scowl at us over the rims of their fingerprint-fogged glasses. They wave their hands like *ignore him*, keep asking us about ourselves.

They've almost always read our work. They compliment our artfulness, that's the word they use, *artful*. They want to recommend us for awards, grants, publications, jobs. When they look at us they see potential. There's this thing that a lot of young writers are doing these days where everything is in the first-person, *I do this I do that*, and they hate it. It's so tactless, self-absorbed. The real writers recognize that we are doing something different.

Some of us are flattered by the attention. Others maybe feel a fibrillation of some clearer, darker instinct. My personal feeling is that I am smart and funny and a good writer, so why don't I deserve to be recognized? Isn't this the way art happens? A dark bar in a strange city, all woozy and electric? Don't I belong here too? The real writers laugh out loud at nearly every joke I make.

They laugh, too, when we leave the bar with them. They laugh like someone has handed them a briefcase full of millions of dollars in unmarked bills.

The real writers put their hands on our thighs, their hands on our hands, their hands on the backs of our heads. They reach out to us when we slip on the ice, or they pull us up when we fall in the grass. They say *Wow* or *You okay?* or *You're too drunk to get home by yourself.* They tip the cab driver generously, like 80 percent.

They fuck us aggressively or tenderly or with childish incompetence. Sometimes we say yes and sometimes we say no but can't tell if they heard us. Sometimes we say no louder and they go *I'm sorry I just have to.* Or *You're just so beautiful.* Sometimes they wait until we are passed out on their couch or their floor or their pilling sheets. Sometimes they don't say anything at all.

No matter what, it always ends. It starts and then it happens and it ends.

We wake up too late in the weak light, quietly pressing our phones to life, *What time is it.* We walk home hungover with two Advil Liqui-Gels in our stomach and droplets of sweat and semen on our inner thighs and something gentle playing in the headphones. The hangover is thick and glassy enough that whatever's happening underneath it is impossible to touch. Not all of us feel good or bad. Not all of us feel anything at all. The city is forgiving in the morning, like you could trust-fall right into it.

When the real writer calls me his girlfriend I think, *Well*. When he says I'm amazing I say, *You literally don't know me at all.* When we are not physically together my phone buzzes and glows with text messages, emails, all day and all night.

Up until now my romantic experience has been limited: a handful of high school boyfriends, a few one-night things with girls who were too cool for me, one chaste but weird high-school romance with a thirty-year-old who lived with his parents. All of those relationships moved at different speeds but had essentially the same structure: the slow-burn crush, the long build-up to the first kiss, the steady climb toward familiarity, each person revealing a little more as time went on. The pace of each escalation was guided by instinct; things happened when they felt like they should happen, or when I decided I wanted them to.

But the real writer moves so fast it's dizzying. Within days of our first night together, he tells me that I am the most beautiful woman he's ever met, the most brilliant, the most fascinating. He remembers every single detail I tell him about my life, no matter how mundane, and frequently repeats them back to me. It is unsettling to be memorized with such force. My grandmother's name sounds strange in his mouth. I sometimes wonder if he's keeping notes.

I'm still taking the antidepressants; they make me unsteady on my feet after one beer. But when I go out with the real writers, who are mostly alcoholics and all at least a decade older than me, I try to keep pace. There is no worse crime than looking immature, or out of place, or like a lightweight, a baby, a child. When someone brings me a shot I take it.

I black out often, something that's never happened to me before. Days start to feel slowed down and sludgy; each night hurtles forward at warp speed. When we wake up together, my body filled with static and my brain with TV snow, I always say, *What happened last night?* When he says, *Don't worry, I remember everything*, I believe it. I have to.

I'm grabbing my ankles in an enormous, freezing cold bar bathroom, breathing hard through my nose, trying to get steady. Or I'm in a pizza place under the harsh light, trying to use the ATM, but I keep pressing the wrong buttons. I'm wearing a huge corduroy jacket that reeks of menthols with a splash of someone's vomit on the arm. I am balancing on the curb while a man's voice says, *I knew you were going to make a big deal out of this*, just outside my field of vision. I'm slipping on the ice. I'm searching through a pile of gum wrappers, beer cans, Starbucks cups, the plastic peeled from packs of cigarettes, for something crucial I can't locate. I'm in my bed on top of a man I barely know. Or I'm lying still with his hands around my breasts and I can't move, I can't move, I can't. Or it's morning and I'm standing in the harsh light of the drugstore, googling *Plan B en francais*, when I get a text that says, *I love you.*

Fighting with him is like stepping into quicksand. We argue over tiny things—whether someone sent a text or said something or showed up when they promised to—but the stakes always feel death-defyingly high. Whenever I try to recount my version of an event, he argues fiercely, insists I'm remembering it wrong, buries me in a barrage of details until I can't find my way out.

The frequency of our arguments is disorienting. Before this relationship I thought I had a good memory, but now I can't seem to get anything right. I wonder what's happening to my brain—whether it's the drinking, the antidepressants, or maybe the same problem that makes me a bad fiction writer, some deeper issue with plot that I'll never be able to fix.

Still, no matter how much I learn to doubt myself, there are memories so strong I can't surrender them. These are often the same ones that make him angriest to hear about, like when I ask whether he remembers the first time we ever had sex—what I said, what he did anyway. His reaction to this question teaches me never to ask it again. Still, I rewind and play through the scene hundreds of times: on the walk home, on the bus, in line for coffee, in classes, in my sleep. It wears through in the places I worry it most.

An afternoon in winter. Mike and I are having lunch. We see each other less lately. I see all my friends less lately, because they are scared to talk to me about my life, and I'm scared to tell them about it. Still, Mike is my best friend and I miss him. I miss sitting on the floor of his apartment, reading together, sharing a mind. I want that feeling back. I want him to tell me that he sees me, that he knows why I'm doing what I'm doing, that it makes sense. The real writer has written me a love poem this week. I hand Mike my phone so he can read it. He squints at the screen for a minute before handing it back.

This is just a list of stuff about you, he says, slowly. His voice is a brick wall.

The real writer and I are out for a walk in the park when we see a woman who looks to be in her mid-fifties on the running path. She notices us, stops and says hi, chats for a bit while jogging in place. After she leaves I go, *Who's that?*

Oh, he says, *that's Sam's wife.* Sam is a professor at the school. I see him out at the bar almost every night, sharing a table with his latest favourite female student, always so close their foreheads are nearly pressed together, whispering about art.

I've never seen him wear a wedding ring, I say, confused.

Well, yeah, he says. *Obviously.*

Sometimes, in class, when I'm really hungover, I daydream about getting someone to drill a small hole at the base of my skull. I imagine my brain dripping out of it like sap while I sit completely still, shoulders square to the blackboard.

Other times, when I'm crossing the street or waiting for the subway, I imagine stepping out onto the road, or jumping down onto the tracks as the train pulls into the station. In this fantasy I am hit so hard that I'm killed almost instantly—but in the moment before I die, I can see everything. All the blacked-out memories I thought I couldn't access were still inside me this whole time, just locked away somewhere I couldn't reach. All I had to do was shake them out.

In the middle of the night, in the stale, freezing air of his apartment, the real writer's phone buzzes and glows. Someone's calling. When he answers, I can hear a woman's voice on the other end of the line, talking very fast. I move toward him and he ducks away. She sounds upset. He rolls out of bed, pads into the other room, speaking in a low whisper. I can still hear her voice. It sounds like *me*, I think. But of course it's not. How could it be?

The real writer breaks up with me at the end of the school year. One of those soft late spring days where everything's just green green green. He picks me up in his car and we idle next to a park while we have the conversation. I stare out the window: people playing tennis, walking their dogs. When he drops me off back at my apartment, he tells me my ass looks good and then disappears. I go upstairs and sit on the balcony. *It's over*, I think. I really think it is.

Several weeks later I discover he is dating a woman who, until very recently, was his student. I cry when I figure it out, cry when I confront him, cry on the street outside the bar in front of all his friends, who watch me with fear and revulsion. I cry on the phone with my mother, cry at the base of the escalators on my way up to class, cry at my friends' houses, cry in my bedroom until I fall asleep, wake up with my cheeks red and my skin creased from the damp, wrinkled pillowcase. I cry until I'm empty, and then I keep crying.

His new girlfriend and I have basically nothing in common. She is a former dancer, quiet and serious, who writes spare short stories about women living alone. I took a class with her once. I said hello to her at readings. She was always friendly with me but I held back. I felt like there was an uncrossable line between us. In a way there was. She'd do shots with us on the real writer's tab. Later, in the cab, he'd say, *I'm worried about that girl, she seems like she's in trouble*, and I'd nod like I knew what he meant. That line between us seemed so real. I could feel it running all the way through me.

Sometimes he still calls me. *Why can't you be an adult about this?* he asks.

I get a summer job at a coffee shop called Café London Bus. The place is downtown, sandwiched between two brutalist office buildings and looking out at an enormous Canadian Tire. We serve between five and ten customers on a good day. In the morning I make sandwiches and scones, plastic-wrap and arrange them carefully in the display case on the counter. In the evening I throw the sandwiches away.

The decor in Café London Bus evokes a UK-themed hospital cafeteria. The café's logo is an anthropomorphized double-decker bus, grinning. In the centre of the dining area there is a large, bright red plastic replica of a British phone booth that fits exactly one chair inside, though I have never seen anyone sit there. On the wall closest to the kitchen there is an enormous flatscreen TV that plays muted footage of a Beatles concert on a loop all day, every day.

The job is not hard, but I'm also not good at it. Like my father before me, I am an abysmal food-service employee: clumsy, prone to long bouts of staring out the window, terrible at small talk in both official languages. My manager, who is also the business's sole proprietor, hates me almost as much as she hates owning the café. In less than a year this place will not exist, but for now the paycheques clear.

I start seeing my real friends again, the ones who are my age. Everyone has started hanging out at a bar in an old auto body shop where they sell tiny hot dogs for cheap. I go to parties in loft buildings that are a tangle of fire hazards: rotting stairways, huge crowds, insufficient exits. I drink corner-store beers on jungle gyms after dark in large, loud groups and bike helmet-less to strangers' houses. I make out with basically anyone who asks. Sometimes I feel it. I'm free.

Halfway through the summer, the real writer sends me a message. My stomach roils when I see his name. His friend, a poet whose work I have loved since before I knew anything else about poetry, runs a small press. They are looking for new young voices to publish, and the real writer recommended me. He explains that he still loves my work and plans to champion it however he can, for as long as I will let him. He says, *Send him some poems.* I say thank you. It seems like the right thing to do.

The poet likes my work. I sell his press my first manuscript and they send me a cheque for about a month's rent. I let my friends take me out to celebrate. I feel good about it, or I know I will feel good eventually.

For the rest of the year, when people ask how I sold my first book so young, I don't know what to say. No matter how much I explain, it always feels like I'm leaving something out. This is, in one sense, the beginning of my career.

In my third year of university I do a study-abroad thing. I sublet my room, pay for the fees and the plane ticket with my parents' money. At my going-away party someone kicks a hole in the drywall of our front hallway while trying to parkour up it. They tape a piece of printer paper over the hole with the words BIG HOLE—WATCH OUT! written in ballpoint pen. I figure it's not really my problem.

I leave for a year. When I come back, everything is almost exactly as I left it, as if no time has passed at all. The same piece of paper with the same words still covers the same hole. The only major change is that the ceiling above my bed is starting to buckle from water damage. It looks terrifying, like it could collapse at any minute. When I ask my roommates about it, they shrug; the landlord stopped answering their calls months ago, though he still cashes their cheques.

My first night sleeping underneath the bowing ceiling, I keep waking up, terrified it's going to fall on me. *There's no way I could possibly ever get used to this*, I think. But eventually I do.

My friends take me back to the hot dog bar, which is a little more crowded than it was last year. I tell them about my time away and then we move on to other topics. A whole year of my life disappears into the humid summer air.

The big news in the city is that the citizens are fighting with the government. Years ago, the premier made a promise that post-secondary education would be free for any citizens of the province who stayed there to get it. Now they're trying to take that promise back, but people do not want to give up their education.

Every evening there are protests. At dusk, all across the city, people come out onto their balconies and bang pots and pans together, singing and hollering and chanting and clapping. Walking through it is stereophonic, lush, unreal.

At the same time, there are demonstrations. The marches move all the way through the city, starting with handfuls of people and ending with hundreds. Some weekends you can take a protest from one neighbourhood to the other like public transit: join in when it stops near your apartment, wander through the crowd as the evening sky turns lavender, bump into a few friends, hop off when you get where you're going.

Through a job website, I get a three-month gig as a copywriter for a medium-sized small music festival. The headquarters are a house that's been half-heartedly converted into an office, but since the first floor is reserved for pop-up vintage clothing sales and concerts, all the employees are crammed in together on the second floor, in what might once have been two bedrooms. The building is not air conditioned, and this summer is uniquely hot.

My job is to write short biographies for the bands and snappy copy for the newsletter. I sit between the festival's original creator and its publicist, who hate each other and bicker poisonously over my head. From my desk, I can see out onto what was once a balcony, but is now just a surface covered in gravel that no one is allowed to walk out onto for insurance-related reasons. There is a toilet sitting out in the middle of the non-balcony, positioned in such a way that my gaze naturally comes to rest on it as I type. I spend my days staring at the toilet as I try to think of new synonyms for "riffs," sipping a watery iced coffee from the bakery down the block, limp breeze from the desk fan intermittently grazing my skin.

I've never written copy for a company before. I like it. I get pleasure and satisfaction from the exercise of speaking as a collective noun. It's cool to think that the idea of the music festival, its "identity," is simultaneously constructed and perpetuated by my work—that I can make it sound more like itself by deciding what it talks like and then making it say what it *would* say if it could. It's not totally unlike writing a poem. I go mostly on instinct. When something feels right I get that feeling again, like I'm disappearing into the text.

The music festival's slush pile is an inbox full of links and mp3s. Most of the bands who play there are famous in a certain way, or friends with the people in charge, but unknown bands from around the world still submit their music in the hopes of landing an opening slot. Every few weeks, festival employees are required to attend "listening parties" to help pick through these unsolicited submissions.

Everyone sits together in a room on the first floor, drinking free room-temperature beer from the festival's sponsors, while the directors play the first three to five seconds of a song. After those few seconds, everyone in the room gives the song a thumbs-up or a thumbs-down. If the response is mostly negative, the band goes in the trash.

A friend asks me to go to a show with her; she has a crush on the bassist in the opening band and doesn't want to show up alone. The headliner is a group I already know and like, a two-piece band famous for playing very, very loudly. One guy plays the drums, and the other shreds guitar and yelps over a fuzzed-out bass synth he plays with his feet. Almost all of their songs are about a lover who does not love the singer back, or maybe many women who have all made him feel the same way, it's hard to tell—she's only ever defined by the negative space she leaves behind.

The lyrics are hard to make out over the crushing volume, but it doesn't really matter. The sound makes a circuit that bypasses language, like the guitar is plugged directly into his mood. I stand at the front of the crowd, right up against the stage. The music is so loud I can feel my organs vibrate.

When the show is over, my friend and I hang around. Eventually someone plugs their laptop into the speakers and everyone starts dancing. When the venue eventually kicks us out, we walk around the city with both bands, laughing. It is one of those shimmering nights where nobody wants to go home. When the sun comes up, I finally start walking back to my apartment. The guitarist comes with me. At my door, he asks if he can come in, and when he finally has to leave he asks for my number. A week later, when their tour is over, he asks if he can come visit me. Before I know it I am falling in love.

When the musician isn't touring he lives in his hometown, a small city halfway between where I live and where I grew up. His city is known for its haunted historical buildings, its university, and its proximity to a maximum-security prison. At night, gangs of engineering students wander the streets in packs, chanting and beating their matching jackets against the pavement.

The musician works in a co-op café and shares a house with a brilliant queer performance artist who's working on a PhD. Their place is beautiful; the artist's collection of vintage taxidermy is tastefully interspersed with the musician's collection of knickknacks and records. An orange Flying V sits plugged into a Marshall stack in the living room. I've never played an electric guitar, but one afternoon when no one else is home I flip the amp on and press the strings against the fretboard. I startle backward when it rings out, shocked by the volume.

I start visiting him every other weekend. To get there I take the cheapest bus line, which is famous for its frequent crashes and explosions. My grandmother mails me newspaper articles from around the world about these buses overturning on highways in bad weather, or getting their tops peeled off like the lid on a tin of anchovies when they pass under low bridges. My experiences are less catastrophic: a guy smokes a full cigarette behind me, or a bus is so oversold that passengers have to sit cross-legged in the aisle for hours, or the engine overheats and sends little wisps of chemical smoke up through the floorboards, so the driver instructs us all to hold the windows open while she drives down the highway at half-speed.

Even after the city opens a brand new shiny white-and-silver bus station with ample seating and generous light, this particular bus company still departs out of a small, dingy room in the ground floor of an office building on the dull edges of downtown. The fabric of the seats is always warm and a little filthy, decorated in purple and royal blue and confetti-points of yellow, like the jazzy design you'd see on a cup of movie-theatre soda from the '90s. If you sit on the lower level you feel as though you are sinking into the belly of the vehicle, travelling in the cargo hold. On the upper level you feel crushed like a can in a recycling machine.

My favourite time to take the bus is late evening on a weekday, near-empty, off-peak. I like watching the sun sink through the filthy windows, no one sitting beside or across from me. I switch my phone to airplane mode and listen to one album in a loop in my headphones, let my brain hum on a setting close to sleep.

The musician seems to know every single person who lives in his city. We run into his friends everywhere we go. They work at the bookstore and the head shop and the record store; they teach at the university or they go to the university; they manage at the artists' co-op or they own the rep cinema. Walking around town with him is like being in a movie with a cast of maybe thirty people. Not one of them knows a single thing about me. It is heaven.

Later, I will remember everything about this time all spliced together, as if the whole year were one continuous scene. Watching a fox dart across the snow-blanketed park up the street from his house. The quiet late-summer walk to the grocery store to pick up lemons and garlic for dinner. Watching *Twin Peaks* at 3:00 a.m. on his mattress on the floor. Eating weed cookies and going to see *Wayne's World* at the cinema and laughing so hard I think I might die. Playing mini golf at the Putt N' Blast in the near-abandoned mall. Bursting into tears outside the Value Village. Watching him watch *The Simpsons* and doing every single line by heart, with perfect timing. Picking records I've never listened to off the shelves in his living room, pulling them out of their sleeves and lowering the needle. When I'm there, this life feels like the only one I've ever lived.

But when I go back to the city I came from, everything is still there, waiting for me.

For example: On the night before the first day of my last year of university, I run into the real writer at a bar. Everything about the evening—the tone of his voice as he tells me he's sorry for what he did, the way he nods to the bartender for another drink, the music of his voice when he says, *You're too drunk to get home by yourself*, the panic coursing through my body when he puts his hands on me—feels so familiar, it's like it never stopped at all.

I sign up for a fiction workshop, because I need another one to complete my degree, and because technically there is still time for me to learn how to write my novel. Mike signs up too, which makes me feel a little better. The professor is a critically acclaimed, award-winning novelist whose Wikipedia page makes me hopeful that he will have some insights about structure and style.

The class is held in the same part of the building where all the real writers have their offices, on the same floor as their literary magazine. The door to its headquarters is almost always open, with the same warm light almost always spilling out.

On workshop days, I wake up with the feeling already sparking in my wrists. It spreads up my arms while I boil the kettle, eat my breakfast, pick out my clothes, nothing too attention-grabbing, nothing too dull. When I leave my apartment, the feeling climbs into my throat, turning my breath into gasping. By the time I climb out of the metro, I can feel it rising to a boil at the top of my skull. I check up and down the block for cars that look like his. I scan the lobby like the Terminator. I take the elevator, power-walk down the hall, not too fast or too slow, in case anyone's looking. I keep my stare locked straight ahead. I duck into the bathroom to breathe. After all this, I usually make it to class.

All this effort turns out to be useless. The critically acclaimed, award-winning professional novelist is usually so monumentally hungover he can barely speak, and the class discusses each other's stories mostly without his assistance.

Everything I write is basically the same. There is a story about a girl who turns into a ghost, a story about a girl who is swallowed by a whale, a girl who takes a radio apart and tries to eat it, piece by piece. The award-winning novelist gives all of them the same grade he gives everyone's work: average, with a few anemic comments in the margins. *I don't think he even reads them,* Mike says, as we throw our work in the trash.

I take a poetry workshop too. Everyone in the class is three years younger than me and already knows each other.

After class, everyone goes out for drinks together. One evening they invite me and I join, feeling clammy and eleven feet tall. At some point everyone's talking about bad relationships and I mention a shitty boyfriend I once had. *There was a bit of an age gap*, I say, on my way to something else, not really thinking. Everyone in the group looks at each other, then at me. The gesture is so perfectly synchronized I must be imagining it. *We know*, someone says, meaning *everyone does*.

All week I'm late for classes, checking my texts, counting down the days. On Friday nights I bolt out of American Postmodern Literature the second it's over, grab a sandwich from the campus café, and run onto the metro with my overnight bag bouncing against my hip.

The musician takes me to the thrift store, the diner, movies, parties, shows. Sometimes he goes to work and I follow him there, spend all day in the café drinking tea and beer and reading books. *Aren't you still in school?* his roommate asks me once, and I am embarrassed, but not enough to take the hint.

One afternoon we are making out in his bed with the windows open, cool air drifting in, late-day light on our faces, when we hear the strains of a brass band drifting in on the breeze. The music is loud, and then it gets louder. I look out the window and realize there is a full parade that has turned off the main street and stopped directly outside the house. They are playing an endless version of "When the Saints Go Marching In" so loudly it's like they're in the room with us. Every time we think it's over and start kissing again, they strike up another verse. I laugh. I can't stop laughing. I laugh so hard I think I am going to leave my body. All around us, the sun streaming in.

One day I am helping the musician go through a bunch of old boxes in his closet. He keeps everything: keys to old houses, notes from old friends, old notebooks full of lyrics and old sketchbooks full of drawings. I love looking at this stuff. I feel like a curator in the museum of him.

The musician has to go do something downstairs for a while. He asks me to flip through the notebooks to check for stuff worth salvaging. I ask whether there's anything private in the pile, anything he doesn't want me to see. He says *No* and I say *Okay* and then he disappears.

His art, like him, is goofy and charming and self-consciously melancholy. One drawing features a forest full of animals all looking dejected—a glum moose, a downcast chipmunk, a tree frowning at the ground. The title of the scene is written in the sky above them: *SAD FOREST.* I set the drawing down in a pile next to some old concert tickets.

Halfway through the box, I come across one notebook that's smaller than the rest. It's red, with an illuminati-eye triangle drawn on the cover. Above it, the musician has written the words *BOOK OF SECRETS* in thick black marker. For a second I feel like I'm watching the protagonist make a crucial decision. Should she read the *BOOK OF SECRETS*? Of course not. But also: How could she stop herself? I understand her decision, even if I don't approve.

Touching the *BOOK OF SECRETS* makes me feel like I am closing a circuit between the past and the present. It is a personal archive and a diary, an art object and a novel. Its original purpose was to document an affair the musician had with the woman he dated before me. Their relationship lasted almost two years. There are scrawled bits of dialogue, notes, sketches, larger scenes rendered in detail.

The love interest in the *BOOK OF SECRETS* is an artist. I recognize her almost immediately as the mythological woman from all of his songs. She is portrayed in tiny glimpses: the feeling of her hair, the mess in her studio. Their relationship is secret and thrilling: they hold hands in the dark, sneak away from their friends, take shortcuts to each other's houses in the middle of the night. They are in love.

At the end of the *BOOK OF SECRETS*, the artist has a show where she presents her thesis to a large audience of peers, friends and teachers. The project is a series of beautifully painted charts where she has meticulously quantified every single thing that's happened in her life for the past four years. Almost everything is accounted for—friends, apartments, classes, parties, relationships—except him. She has excised their affair completely. The narrator sits there quietly, watching her present the story of her life, the one that does not include him, marinating in his pain and isolation. It hurts to be made invisible.

It is frustrating when your desires conflict with the intentions of the narrator. I want to know why the artist has chosen to tell the story of her life this way, but the musician never asks her. The book just cuts off there, like it's the end.

About halfway through the year, I start trying to write a new poem for my workshop, but I can't figure out how. I wonder whether I have lost the ability to write poems entirely, or whether I ever had it at all. I am trying to say something about narrative, but I can't make it cohere.

I spend hours staring into this poem. I move ideas around the way you'd shuffle furniture in an ugly apartment, trying to cover up the most obvious flaws. I change the language, the tense, the perspective, the names, the themes, the shape, the form. I add speakers and take them away. For a while I insert the image of an enormous pile of recycling that glows like a cartoon pile of nuclear waste, just to make things interesting.

I bring the poem in to workshop and no one likes it. *It kinda feels like you don't know what this is yet*, says one of my classmates, who is correct. *I don't ever write about anyone*, the speaker in the poem says to her boyfriend, in a passage I keep deleting and retyping. *It seems like planting your flag in the sea.*

At the end of the year, the small press publishes my first book of poems. I throw the launch party in an art gallery, because it is not a reading series or a bar.

The book is a beautiful object, exactly the right size and weight. The cover is perfect. When I read my own name on the spine I feel a distant sense of pride, like you would for a cousin who just got a promotion. *Good for her.* School is ending and I need a job.

Every day I scour the online listings, write cover letters and email them into the void. I've looked for work before, but never at this pace or pitch, and I feel surprised by the ease with which I churn out variations on the same few dull sentences over and over. *I have experience creating and managing a broad range of written content. I have experience in customer service roles. My responsibilities included liaising between members of the public and upper management. Proficient in Microsoft Office. Punctual, responsible, eager to learn.* The more I write, the easier these phrases flow through me. It's like discovering a language inside me I didn't know I could speak.

I get a few responses—software developers, game developers, tech companies whose products I don't understand. After class, I smear on foundation under the fluorescent lights of the university bathroom and practice my professional smile. I take the metro out to far-flung neighbourhoods to write copyediting tests in grim windowless rooms. I talk to HR managers about missions, content, peers, security. I nod until my neck is sore. No one ever calls me back.

Most of the people I know in this city work at bars, or in tele-marketing centres, or selling their underwear to strangers on the internet. But lately another theme is starting to emerge.

In a café, a friend of a friend tells me she works night shifts at a 24/7 call centre for the billing department of a popular website that specializes in hardcore anal sex. The job, she says, mostly involves fielding calls from angry wives and mothers, all from the American South for some reason, who want to know what this charge is doing on their husband's or son's credit card bill.

At a reading, an artist tells me she quit her last café job to start doing webcam shows. The site that hosts her videos takes a large percentage of her tips, and the work can be tedious, but she makes five times what she used to and doesn't come home reeking of coffee.

At a party, the host's roommate tells me she just quit her job, which was to sit in an office and watch porn scenes for eight hours a day. Her whole thing, she says, from nine to five, was to watch videos on fast forward and note down the exact time at which any given performer entered or exited a scene. She knew it was time to quit, she tells me, the first time she recognized an actor *by his nutsack first.*

At a bar, a professional translator tells me she also writes copy for the "VIP blog" of a porn site. Her job is to build a world around the idea that the magazine employs four or five outland-ishly hot, perpetually horny women who write the exact same way they talk, and who love nothing more than recommending links to content from other, affiliated websites. In her blog posts she pushes keywords and videos to the top of the company's page three or four times a day, embedding the website further and further inside of itself.

At a show, a friend's new boyfriend tells me he's trying to break into the scriptwriting business. There's a porn production company, he says, that takes scripts from anybody who can write them. You send them your script, and if they like it enough to use it, they drop a few hundred dollars in your bank account, no questions asked. *You really only have to write the beginning and the end,* he says. Since he started writing these scripts he's noticed himself mentally measuring every situation for its potential to become pornographic. At the grocery store, at the dentist, at band practice—he looks around and thinks, *Could everyone here plausibly just start fucking?*

I don't actually remember the first time I ever watched porn. When I was a teenager, our house had one computer—a cheerful bright blue plastic iMac that lived in the spare room at the top of the stairs. I was addicted to MSN Messenger and, weirdly, the forums for a free-form radio show based out of Jersey City, which I had discovered on LiveJournal and now listened to faithfully every evening while I did my homework.

My mother was appropriately anxious about my internet use, so her solution was to implement a transparency rule: I had to keep the office door open whenever I was using the computer, so she could glance in and check what I was doing at any time. When I started to need my own computer for assignments in high school, she bought me a refurbished MacBook—a big shiny white plastic square, like an oversized Chiclet—from which the wi-fi card had been surgically removed. If I wanted to cruise the information superhighway, I had to plug my laptop into the very short Ethernet cable in the office and keep the door behind me open.

None of this, of course, kept me from looking up porn. Instead, it turned the process into a high-stakes stealth mission. Our house was ancient: the walls were paper-thin, the hardwood floor creaked like music. Sound carried so clearly through the vents that if my mother was rehearsing lines in the basement I could hear it in my bedroom, and if my stepfather was watching hockey in the living room I always knew the score. Awareness of other people's activities was like a sixth sense: ambient, bodily, impossible to switch off.

Usually I'd wait until my mother and stepfather were out in the backyard, or stationed on the couch watching TV. When I was sure they were distracted, I'd bring my laptop into the office and nearly close the door. Subtle and quiet as a bag full of live raccoons, I'd yank the Ethernet cable out of the computer and plug it into my laptop. Then I'd literally just google the word "porn" and frantically right-click to download as many clips of whatever came up until my mother came inside or up the stairs. When I heard her approaching, I'd slam the lid of my laptop as casually as possible, replug the cable, run back to my room, and wait until she was downstairs again to open up the laptop. Then—face glowing like I was looking into a briefcase full of priceless treasure—I'd sort through what I'd found.

These videos were pixelated, and often played for only forty seconds before glitching or sputtering out. Their content was about what you'd expect from the first page of search results for "porn" in the early 2000s. The women were exclusively white and had almost no visible body hair. Their nails were immaculately manicured and sharpened to painful-looking points; they masturbated with a flat-palmed style that fascinated me but that I could not replicate to any practically useful effect. Watching the way men handled their bodies lit a lush panic in my lower gut—kaleidoscopic, neon-edged.

The first few times I watched these videos, I was excited and terrified by what I was seeing. But after a while, the thrill settled into something like comfort. The scenes I watched were almost always the same, and the feelings they evinced became equally predictable. The performers' bodies always ended up in two or three identical positions, and the phrases they moaned or muttered always seemed to have been picked off a master list.

I was maybe twelve or thirteen years old, and though I had not yet even kissed another person I knew that everything on earth was, in some way, about sex. Rarely mentioned directly but constantly referred to, sex was a force whose promise and threat controlled most of what my friends and I were allowed or not allowed to do. I knew it was somehow at the heart of my mother's regulations about the computer, and my friends' parents' rules about what they could wear, and everyone's fears about what we were listening to on the radio and seeing on TV. Even in my own thoughts I could sense its push and pull, a powerful tension that excited and scared me, but that I could rarely gather into a coherent idea or fantasy. Sex was just always *there*—as in everywhere, ineffable and ubiquitous as oxygen.

Porn made it literal, took the mystery away. In the videos I watched, sex was never mysterious or subtextual—it was the plainly inevitable outcome of every possible situation. Every human interaction steered toward it, unfolded according to its rhythms, and ended when the guy came. It was a relief to see the invisible driver of all things turned concrete, corralled into such a simple structure, laid out in a narrative line. Beginning, middle, end. Realer than real.

The porn company's office is in a part of town I've never visited. The escalator leading out of the metro station is unusually long and steep, even for a city where all the subways feel incredibly underground. Above the escalator floats a cloud of enormous concrete sculptures: cubes shaped like dice and lined with lit fluorescent tubes, suspended from the ceiling. I get so distracted staring at them that I almost fall off when the escalator reaches the top.

Between the metro station and the office there is a strip club and a motel and eight very dangerous lanes of traffic. In the distance, I can see a Walmart and a 24-hour Harvey's and an ancient Orange Julius, shaped like an actual orange, all rising out of the bleak, brutalist landscape. The porn building is short, wide, and made entirely of dark, mirrored glass. It rises up over the expressway, shimmering like a supervillain's lair, repeating the dull grey of the highway below and the slate sky wrapped around it.

The second I step inside, an enormous, square-shaped security guard in a dark blue blazer stands up from behind the front desk to stop me from going any farther. After I explain why I'm there he signs me in; another guard, exactly the same shape and size, escorts me toward the elevator, pressing a badge to a scanner that opens the door.

I step out into a hallway that smells like fresh paint and sawdust. Everything is lit like an Apple store: bright white, relentless. I keep catching my own reflection in the glass doors of the meeting rooms we pass. The guard ushers me into a reception area. It's empty except for a few chairs and an enormous reception desk. There is a woman sitting behind it, with a video screen behind her. The guard gestures to a chair; I sit down, and he disappears.

From this angle, there is nowhere for me to look except at the video screen. I feel self-conscious, worried the receptionist will think I am staring at her, but she betrays absolutely no sign that she even notices I'm there. The screen behind her plays a series of slides:

****** is an international information technology firm, specializing in highly trafficked websites. The company creates, develops and manages some of the most recognized mainstream and adult entertainment brands in the world. As an uncontested market leader, ****** has developed various in-house technologies with respect to HD video streaming and website optimization, which enables it to compete on a matchless playing field. Headquartered in Luxembourg with management offices in Hamburg, London, Los Angeles, Nicosia, and Montreal, the company employs over 900 people.

I'm so mesmerized by the words' slow drift across the screen that when, eventually, a woman in an A-line skirt suit and perfect makeup with immaculately blow-dried hair appears in my field of vision, she seems to have melted backward into the reception area from out of the wall. She takes me back toward the elevators, past another security guard. We step in together and she pushes the button for a lower floor. *This is where you'll be working if you get the position,* she says, as the doors open.

This floor of the office is different from the others. It's as if we have travelled back in time about fifteen or twenty years to an entirely different type of workplace: instead of a bright

white, open space, there is an endless warren of cubicles, pho-
tocopiers, printers, desks, rough wall-to-wall carpeting, grey
on white on beige on grey. The woman leads me through the office.
I can see porno-
graphy on nearly every computer screen I pass, but I barely
notice the content; instead, I'm shocked by how many screens
everyone seems to be using at once. Each workstation has at
least two monitors, and their inhabitants lean toward them
while staring down into their phones. I see people playing
games and managing chats and clipping video all at once, tapping each keyboard with one hand, one eye on each screen, all
that blue light making their faces glow.

The woman steers me into a conference room where a thin
man in a loose soccer jersey and nylon pants sits in a low office
chair, aggressively swiping at an iPad that dings and buzzes
back at him every forty-five seconds or so. He barely acknowledges our presence. As the woman talks, she betrays almost
no sign that she notices the sounds and the swiping—except
that every so often, after a particularly long string of dings and
buzzes, her eyes close in a tiny, involuntary wince.

She asks me some questions about my resume, tells me a
few basic things about the job, and, when she is done talking,
shoots the man in the corner a significant look. *I don't know
much about the technical stuff you'll be doing, so our IT expert can
get into it with you,* she says. I feel a light wash of panic rising in
me. I don't know much about it either.

The IT expert looks up from his iPad, as if only now noticing that I have entered the room. *Got any big questions?* he asks,
and before I can even think the word yes, he begins telling me
about his own history as a technical writer, and before that, as

a writer of everything. He lists multiple degrees and a number of instruction manuals, articles, essays, pamphlets, so many kinds of work I lose track. *That's impressive,* I say at an appropriate time, and he shakes his head. *It's not. I'm just good at writing,* he says. *It's what I do.*

On the table between us, there is a copy of my resume. The IT expert picks it up and glances at it, and I can see the shadow of a few lines: *CREATIVE WRITING, CAFÉ, STANDARDIZED.* It feels weird to see those words in this room, to think of other people reading those phrases and printing them out, trying to assess me. He lays the resume face down on the desk and looks at me over his glasses. "Have you ever been a technical writer before?"

"No," I say, feeling reasonably confident that this will be the end of the interview.

"That's great," he says. "Good. Great. I like it. You're mould-able." I don't know what shape my face is making but whatever it is, he immediately rushes to correct himself. "It's not a bad thing. It just means you'll do this job the way we need you to do it." I try to hold my face as still as possible, no longer sure what it's betraying.

After the interview, he takes me back down to the lobby, swiping his security badge as a security guard's eyes follow him reflexively. In the elevator, petrified of the silence, I ask why there are so many guards everywhere.

"They're all ex-cops. Military guys. That kind of thing," he says. A long, confusing silence passes between us; the elevator drops a few floors. "This business used to be very different," he says, presumably by way of explanation. I search my brain for job-interview-appropriate responses to this statement, but the doors open before I can find one. "We'll call you," the IT expert says cheerfully, waving a little as I step back out into the world.

The first time I ever had sex was with my high school boyfriend. I was sixteen years old and my family was out of town. It was our one-year anniversary. I set the dining room table for us the same way I did for family dinners—place mats, candles, big wooden salad bowl. After we ate an awkward, silent meal a thousand feet apart, I led him upstairs.

We made a real effort, about which I can remember nothing except that my antique bedframe's rusted springs sagged and creaked so loudly I thought the whole thing was going to fall apart. After ten or fifteen minutes, we both laid back and looked up at the ceiling for a few seconds before glancing sideways at each other.

Eventually he broke the silence: *So... that's it?*

I was hurt, but also I knew exactly what he meant. I had spent so much time thinking about sex—imagining it, testing and measuring for it in every conversation—that I'd somehow forgotten to account for the fact that it was going to happen to my body. The whole thing had been uncomfortably *physical*: I'd been so conscious of my limbs, my racing heart, my sparking brain. Every single part of me felt obvious, enormous, inflexible. Plus it hurt.

We kept trying. Books and the internet and a few of my friends told me it would stop hurting after I'd had a little practice, but it felt the same every time—not painful enough to stop, but enough to take me entirely out of the moment, override any pleasure. I felt certain that this was a failure on my part, something I wasn't doing or doing too much. I thought that if I just worked hard enough, I'd be able to learn how to leave my body the same way I did when I was in my bedroom alone, watching videos of other people fucking. But no matter how much I tried, things stayed the same.

I knew, intellectually, that sex was not supposed to hurt. My mother had always told me that sex should be a pleasurable, safe exchange with someone you trusted; I had read the same thing in books and on forums late at night, when I tried to search for solutions to my problem. But in the back of my mind, I still wondered whether the pain I was experiencing was more common than anyone wanted to admit. If heterosexual sex always caused the woman some kind of pain, it would explain some of the messages I'd been absorbing in popular culture. In books and movies, television and songs, sex was often portrayed as a chore or a sacrifice, something straight women gave away or withheld as part of the broader negotiation of their relationships with men. Maybe, I thought, this was the truth every adult woman knew, but that no one wanted to articulate completely: that no matter how good it felt, sex always kind of hurt you.

Eventually, my doctor sent me to a specialist who worked out of a hospital downtown, a building I'd only ever been in for Standardized Patient exams. My appointment was on a grim mid-winter day. The hospital was nearly empty; I was the only person in the waiting room. I remember looking around at the rows of empty plastic seats and feeling entirely untethered from the present—like when the doctor came to get me, I'd have no way of knowing if he was a student or a professional, playing a role or performing a job.

I had never seen a male gynaecologist before. When he touched my stomach and said my bladder seemed full, I thought of the way the vet had remarked on our cat's full stomach the last time we took him in for a check-up. The exam was long and painful. At the end of it, the specialist told me he had no idea what the cause of my pain was, but that the pain I was feeling was common and would likely go away on its own eventually. He could not give me any more concrete advice, he said, since the cause could be any number of things. If it got worse, I should come back. In the meantime, he could prescribe me a cream that would numb the area, so that when I had sex I wouldn't have to feel anything at all.

I took the prescription and never filled it. Instead, I just got good at faking orgasms. At first, I was just copying the broad outlines of what I'd seen women do in porn—close your eyes, make a lot of noise, shake a little—but the more I practiced, the more natural they felt. By the time my boyfriend and I broke up, I'd faked it so often that the gesture had begun to imprint itself alongside the other reflexive, routine gestures of sex. These kinds of orgasms rose out of my body as naturally as the real ones I experienced alone, in bed or in front of the computer.

The more I practiced, the more rich and complex the experience became—a gesture that felt as intimate and linked to my feelings as the thing it was pretending to be. I faked orgasms as punctuation, as a compliment, as a cheap and frictionless method of self-defence. Each time I did it, I experienced a heady rush of pride and guilt that gave the experience depth and dimension. I felt like I'd invented a way to describe without words a condition that normal language was inadequate for; something about pleasure and pain pushing and pulling, neither experience overriding the other. A reflex. Bodily, like any other.

On my first day of work, there's a raging downpour that lasts exactly as long as it takes me to walk from the metro station to the office. I arrive at the introductory meeting on time, dripping wet, and dead last. The boardroom's walls are glass, so everyone can see me coming. The rest of this month's new recruits are sitting around a long table. Everyone has a maroon folder in front of them embossed with the company's logo, a big stylized letter M. Everyone stares at me. Rain rolls down my forehead and across my face like cartoon drops of sweat.

I plonk down into the only available seat. The man next to me is wearing a fresh suit, and when I feel him shift away I resist the urge to shake myself off like a wet dog. Instead, I open my folder and glance inside at the contents: a sheaf of contracts, a branded pen, a lanyard. Before I have the chance to read any of it, a woman at the head of the table stands up, smooths out her skirt, clears her throat, and introduces herself as a representative of the HR department. She asks us to open our folders, and begins to deliver a presentation about the history of the company we are about to join.

It is the most engaging PowerPoint I will ever see in my life. The HR rep recites its contents in a brisk, professional tone that betrays absolutely no hint of emotion but does suggest she has to give this speech a lot. The slides behind her move swiftly through a decade of corporate history, from the company's humble origins in a university dorm room all the way up to its present state, recently purchased by an international billionaire and dominating the world of internet pornography. The story of this company could be the plot of a Hollywood blockbuster, but the language of the presentation smooths it down to near-dullness. As the PowerPoint chugs along, I think to myself that an immaculately coiffed business executive describing the genesis of a billion-dollar porn company like she's talking about the invention of a frozen-yogurt franchise will probably be the closest thing to performance art I'll see today. But I am wrong. That part comes right at its end, when the screen behind the HR exec fills with a slide containing a complete list of the websites the company currently owns:

Brazzers, Reality Gang, 3D Xstar, Mofos, Babes, Twistys, Webcams, Moviebox, Men.com, JuicyBoys, DigitalPlayground, PornHub, Youporn, Tube8, Xtube, ExtremeTube, Spankwire, KeezMovies, GayTube, and *TrafficJunky* (plus the non-porn video content sites *LolThis* and *SuperHippo*).

She recites this list in exactly the same tone she has used for the rest of her speech, level and unsuggestive, in the kind of cadence a weather reporter might use to recite the fourteen-day forecast. It is a transcendent performance.

For the next decade of my life, I will keep the maroon folder with my other important papers—tax records, signed contracts—and every so often I'll pull it out, handling it by the edges as though it were a precious archival document. I'll flip past the descriptions of our employee benefits (free hot breakfast once a week!) and perks (20 percent off at a mall coffee shop if you show your lanyard!), past the office codes of conduct (no spaghetti straps!), and return to this list. Each time I read it, I will learn something new about language. The unbreakable chain from one word to another, from each name to the next, from the collection of titles to the world it evokes.

When her presentation is done, the HR exec introduces the IT expert, who she says will be delivering a lecture about "the technical side of things." He is wearing the exact same outfit as the last time I saw him. He does not have a PowerPoint presentation; instead, he launches into an improvised monologue, describing the company's scope and reach in a barrage of metrics for which I have no frame of reference.

All I understand is that it seems like *a lot*. A lot of people are visiting these websites every day, a lot of videos are streamed and downloaded each month. Years of data passing through decades of cable, of air. The company, he tells us, has multiple massive servers all over the globe to help them handle all this traffic. *So if there's ever, say, a huge earthquake in California and the whole state falls into the ocean, we can just failover to our servers in Amsterdam like that*—he snaps his fingers—*and no one watching our videos would ever know a thing.* The thought of someone blissfully jerking off, unaware that the world is literally falling apart because of flawless video playback, makes me snort-laugh. I try to cover it up, but the IT expert pauses his speech for a fraction of a second that lets me know he heard me. I wonder how long I will last at this job.

After we get our ID photos taken, the IT expert leads me through the floor of the office I remember from my interview. After the glass-walled boardroom, the space feels especially humid and cramped. It smells like recycled air and wet men. The sound is low ambient chatter plus typing, the light is harsh and dull and even, and the carpet is that elementary-school kind; grey and gritty and strung through with thread that feels like fishing wire.

My desk is a long table with two computer monitors on it, surrounded by piles of cardboard boxes. There are boxes on either side of the desk, on the floor around the chair. *You're the first person we've hired for this position,* my new boss explains, shrugging. He explains the email system and says my staff login gives me access to all of the company's websites for free. Then he leaves me alone to "get acquainted with the brand." I spend the rest of the day with six different porn websites open on my two monitors, glancing surreptitiously over my shoulder and switching over to social media when I don't think anyone's looking.

My job is to write instruction manuals for computer programs I don't understand. For years, the porn company has been developing software to manage things like video playback and advertising on its websites, and now they are planning to sell this technology to other companies. They need instruction manuals for these programs: straightforward, understandable, free of both technical jargon and authorial voice.

On my third day of work, the IT expert gives me my first piece of busywork: converting a messy paragraph of text written by a software developer into plain, readable English. The task takes me a few days to complete. I spend a lot of time searching technical terms I don't recognize, and even more anxiously fantasizing about what my boss will say when he realizes I am entirely unqualified for my job. When I can't put it off any longer, I email him my work. *Thanks*, he replies. *More soon.* I never hear about the assignment again.

This sets the pattern. About once a week I am given a task, which I finish in a day or two and fire off into the void. Then I spend the rest of my time in the office clicking around Twitter, with an emergency window of hardcore pornography ready in the taskbar in case my boss should walk up behind me and glance at my screen. He never actually does, but the feeling brings me back to sitting in my mother's office, laptop plugged into the Ethernet cable, ready to bolt.

Weeks pass like this. I'm not sure what I'm supposed to be doing with all my free time, or whether I am eventually going to get in trouble for having so much of it. Should I be alerting someone to the fact that I have nothing to do? Or should I just accept the situation for what it is—the opportunity to be paid for doing nothing—and be grateful?

The IT expert seems to remember I work there, but doesn't appear to notice how little I do. Every time I see him he's tapping away at his iPad, completely engrossed. Each day he wears a different novelty T-shirt, the kind you see at mall stands or gas stations, printed with needlessly confrontational slogans. One of my favourites says, IF I'M TALKING . . . YOU SHOULD BE TAKING NOTES. Another says, across the front, I'D LOVE TO HELP YOU, then on the back: BUT I CAN'T FIX STUPID!

The more I interact with him, the more I wonder whether I was really hired to write instruction manuals, or whether my true job is just to absorb his wisdom. Our department meetings are the only time he ever really addresses me directly; in the middle of talking about a project, he'll turn to me and, as if there is no one else in the room, begin telling me about his career.

Writing comes naturally to me, he says during one of these monologues, with the faraway gaze of someone being interviewed for posterity. *It always has. I'm a person that can write. It's not impressive. It's just what I'm good at.* I'm not sure whether I should be writing down what he says or looking up at him with my full attention while he gives these speeches, so I try to do both at the same time. When I look down at the end of the meeting, my notes are completely unintelligible.

I know a few other people who work in the office—mostly poets with copywriting jobs—but I hardly ever see them. The company, we are always being reminded in memos and emails, employs thousands of people and is ever growing, constantly expanding its horizons.

What these notes never explain is how it got so big in the first place. Over the past several years, the company has bought up a vast share of the pornographic websites across the internet and assimilated them into its sprawling, networked ecosystem. Now it effectively controls the production and distribution of almost all the mainstream porn on the internet.

The Tube sites in particular—some of the company's most high-traffic properties, where users can upload and watch videos for free—represent a near-infinite library of endlessly recirculating content, thoroughly tagged and indexed by genre, performer, and any other data imaginable. Once a video is uploaded to one of these sites it becomes incredibly difficult to pull down; even if someone files a copyright claim, the video can be shared, saved, screenshotted, downloaded, and reposted before it's pulled. Once a piece of content falls into this endless churn, it's essentially surrendered to the company. For people who once made a living producing and performing in their own porn, the choice is bleak: You can work for the company, accepting however much they offer to pay you, or you can try to stay separate from them and risk your work being rendered valueless in just a few clicks.

All day long, while I sit at my desk refreshing Twitter, the company humming away at my back is hard at work methodically chewing up and spitting out an entire creative industry, bulldozing the precarious structures that have allowed a class of workers to make a living off their labour for decades. Reporters will write about this double bind in the years after the company has bled the industry dry, and performers will speak out about it at great risk to their careers. But while I work there, the extent of its monopoly has not yet been publicized, and I'm not curious enough to wonder what the corporation whose name is on my paycheques actually does to generate their money. Working there does not make me think more deeply about the videos

I've spent my whole adult life watching, or the conditions that delivered them to me in the first place.

In fact, it makes me more callous. One night, at a party, I am using my job as an entertaining story. At one point I say loudly that I work *inside the beating heart of the patriarchy*, and most people laugh; a few men even ask me sympathetic questions about what that must be like for me. But in my peripheral vision I notice one woman—a friend of a friend who has done webcam shows for money—rolling her eyes. I can tell she understands something about my job that I don't, so for the rest of the night I avoid her.

Time passes. Maybe a couple months. Every morning, as I wade through rows of cubicles and workstations to get to my own, I can hear the hum of every monitor. When I sit down at my desk I can feel their glow throwing a sickly heat against my skin.

I eat lunch on a bench outside, sometimes alone, sometimes with the other poets. Sometimes I walk around the expansive Jewish cemetery a few blocks from the office, my eyes straining to focus on the headstones after hours of glazed-over staring at screens.

When I come back inside, the air always feels heavy; I wonder whether the sawdust from the construction on other floors could be coming through the vents, settling in my lungs. I text my friends *Wouldn't it be funny if I got an old-timey illness just from working in this office? Porn lung?* I download a game on my phone where you connect dots to other dots that are the same colour; if you can make them into a square, your phone vibrates and makes a little noise. I play this game so often I see it imprinted on the blackness when I close my eyes, feel it moving in my hand when there's nothing there. I take twenty-minute bathroom breaks, sitting on the toilet with the lid down, hunched over my tiny screen, making the shapes and then making them disappear. No one notices my absence. By the time I come home at the end of the day I feel like I am looking at myself through a thick pane of glass.

The office is uncannily hard to remember. Even though I spend hours sitting in the same place, staring at the same screen, walking up and down the same hallways, riding in the same elevator, searing the space into my memory, the second I leave for the day all those images start to degrade. On weekends I can barely remember what any of it actually looks like. Trying to describe even the most basic physical details of the office—the colour of the carpets, the walls, the monitors—I find myself struggling to separate the real from the imaginary, my actual office from the images of offices I've looked at in TV and movies for years. So many things about the space feel like I could have made them up or seen them somewhere—either because they're so normal, or because they're so strange.

This will present a problem for me years later, when the job has turned from an experience into a memory and then into a story. I will rely on photos, small souvenirs, the notes I took in emails, to remember what this place was like and what I did there. Some of my memories are so specific that I feel certain they must be true, or else that they're impossible; it's hard to tell the difference.

In one of these scenes, I'm sitting in the office late at night. The building is open twenty-four hours a day, and the company allows us to come in and leave whenever we want as long as we stay for our requisite eight. A couple months in I started showing up later and later, and now I am trapped in a cycle of bad timing: I wake up late, shovel some burned oatmeal into my mouth, pull on my dissolving thrift-store shoes, barrel out the door, travel underground to a new part of the city where the largest marker is the building constructed to look like an enormous orange. I head into a building made out of sky, swipe my pass in front of an unsmiling phalanx of identical fake cops. I go to my desk and refresh the same three websites until the sun sets and my brain feels like a pulsing pile of radioactive slush inside my skull. The air around me is textured with the sounds of performative fucking. A few hours later I leave unacknowledged, invisible as a ghost.

The cardboard boxes that surrounded my computer on the first day are still there. In fact, it feels like they multiply overnight each time I leave. There are boxes stacked on the ground and along any unused desk space on either side of my workstation. Each box is roughly the same size as every other, and all of them are closed. Still, when no one is looking, I sometimes open one of them and check out what's inside. Each box is different; one might be full of reams of plain white printer paper, while another, stacked on top of it, is full of promotional DVDs for a film called *Honey, I Fucked the Babysitter.*

On this one evening it's so late there's no one else in the office, a rare occurrence. For a second I think I can hear another person typing, and then I realize that it's just the sound of my own clacking keyboard echoing off the high ceiling. Past my monitor, I can see out the window. Traffic on the highway has slowed to a hush. I check the time and realize I still have another hour and a half before I can leave. I put my feet up on the box before me on the floor and open another tab.

Suddenly, without looking, I know there's someone behind me. They're all the way across the office, but I can feel them— like an animal in the forest who knows another animal. The hairs on the back of my neck stand up. My spine stiffens. I can't move.

For a few seconds it's quiet. I wonder if I was imagining it. But then I hear footsteps on the carpet, getting closer. My whole body is tensed, my shoulders up around my ears. By the time I hear a man clear his throat behind me I have to gulp back a yelp.

When I turn, I am face to face with a security guard. He looks both determined and a little nervous. Shy? I am unused to reading expression on the guards' faces, because it is part of their job not to betray any. I sit there looking up at him. I can feel my pulse in the back of my skull, inside my wrists. Finally, after what feels like an hour of silence, he points toward my feet, at the cardboard box where they are resting. He asks me whether he can open it. "The guy told me . . ." he says in a thick French Canadian accent, shrugging the end of the sentence away.

I feel a flush of relief so strong it makes me tender. I want very badly to help this man get what he needs. I pull the box out from under my feet and push it toward him. He nods at it, but not at me, kneels down to open it, and takes something out of the box. He closes the lid, stands up and walks away quickly before I have the chance to see what he's holding. When he's far enough away, I bend down and peer inside the box. It is full of novelty Fleshlights, zombie-themed.

Almost every day after work, I go to the thrift store. It's a ten-minute walk from the office, but for some reason it always feels much longer—maybe because it takes me down a sidewalk next to a highway off-ramp, cars whipping by so fast and close I feel like I'm doing a death-defying tightrope walk.

The thrift store is my favourite place in the world. It feels like a church: tall ceilings, floors polished to a high gloss, piped-in music so airy you can practically breathe it. The racks of clothes are so perfectly arranged I feel like a criminal touching them. For some reason, no one's ever here—at least not on weekday evenings.

Every time I visit, I find something that fits so neatly into my life it feels like it already belongs to me. An orange Le Creuset pot that matches a piece my grandmother gave me. A white antique radio that fits perfectly into an empty spot on my kitchen shelf. A silk leopard print dress that slips over my body like water. I feel like I'm compiling something: a collection, an archive, a database. The more I find, the more I have to visit.

The music section is perfect, too—the records are never picked over, and there are always new gems to collect. I am building a collection of 45s, all love songs. Together they form an index of metaphor: love is like a baseball game, like a fashion show, like a dream, a possession, a memory. Love makes you call someone's house over and over again until their brother picks up and tells you they're not home, love keeps you waiting by the telephone in your apartment for weeks, love is eternal but always contains a glimmer of its own eventual loss. I like the infinite variations—how each song is about the same thing as every other, yet always completely new.

When I get something really good I send a picture of it to the musician, who knows more about records than anyone I've ever met. Whenever I ask him what he thinks of a song he has an immediate answer. The synths in this one sound like a swarm of golden bees descending from heaven and wrapping around you; the MC in that one sounds like he is talking to you from inside a spaceship hovering above your house. After he describes a song to me I listen to it again, comparing my impressions to his, taking note of where they overlap or diverge. If I do this enough, I lose track of which opinion is mine.

Our relationship is mostly good. In the evenings, after dinner, I lie on my horrible second-hand couch and phone him to ask about his day. Now that he's off tour, the musician shuttles between long days at the café and late-night rehearsals. Everything takes a toll on his body. Sometimes while he's practicing guitar his hand goes completely numb from carpal tunnel. Other days, after a run of shifts in the kitchen, his back hurts so much he can barely get out of bed. When it is really bad and he still has to work, he fills a rubber glove with ice cubes and shoves it under the waistband of his pants to numb the pain running up his spine. Whenever he asks me about my day I think of the hours I spent sitting in a chair, clicking on nothing for a salary that exceeds his hourly pay, and feel deeply ashamed.

On weekends when I can't visit him, I go out drinking with my friends. When I come home I inevitably call him and pick an apocalyptic fight about anything—something he texted me or failed to text me, something he said a week ago, something he did that day without me. The next morning, I wake up paralyzed with shame, call him with apologies tumbling out of my mouth like pennies from a slot machine. Neither of us knows what exactly is happening in these exchanges. It feels like my behaviour is being operated by someone who lives outside my body, whose motivations and desires I cannot understand.

When we have sex, it's always different. Sometimes when he touches me a dull roar starts in the roof of my mouth and moves through my whole body until I'm made of TV static. Other times I get a piercing stomachache that doesn't stop until I can lie down on my back in the dark alone. Or I can taste the stale air of the office on my tongue, or I can feel the rough sheets of another bed under my back, or I can sense the true purpose of my life under the surface, moving my hands across his body like the pointer on a Ouija board. Later, in the dark, I can feel it slithering across my throat, leaving a glowing trail across my skin.

I never feel turned on at work, although I am surrounded by videos of people having sex in every conceivable position and arrangement. I think often of an interview I read with a guy who worked at the mint printing money. *If people can work here for five days and still see this as currency,* he said, *they shouldn't work here anymore.*

I still try to watch porn at home, more out of a reflexive compulsion than a real desire. Usually it happens after I come home from work and spend a couple hours picking at my novel—opening the document, changing a word, removing a comma, putting it back again—or working on an application for a grant or a residency I'm certain I won't receive. I close the window feeling like a criminal, and then I open up my browser.

Often, I end up watching the videos of an extremely popular straight couple. They are conventionally attractive and good at their jobs. The two of them have become so famous they're each teetering on the edge of their own mainstream celebrity—she as a writer, he as an actor. They both perform rough scenes—the man likes to hit women, choke them, force them to the ground—but unlike a lot of other videos on the Tube sites, it's easy to believe their scenes are completely consensual. The woman laughs brightly when she seems turned on. The man is aggressively focused on generating female orgasms. Watching the two of them have sex—with each other or with other people—feels like you're being let in on a secret, something real.

The couple's influence is profound. Nearly all the men I have sex with for the next decade will, at some point, let slip a gesture that reveals their study of the man's techniques. You can hear his voice inside the way they growl or whisper, his signature phrases coming through their clenched teeth.

A few years from now, after the couple breaks up, fans will still be posting photos of the two of them together, leaving comments on their videos about how they aspire to be fucked the way he fucked her. Eventually, she will write a thread explaining that he violated her safe words and her consent multiple times, that he had sex with her after she said *stop* and *no*. After she does this, other women will come forward with their own stories about the man. The details will vary, but the central themes will be so similar they'll sound like they all happened to the same person.

He will, of course, deny everything. A few producers will stop working with him, but eventually the story will fade and his career will pick back up. Sometimes his videos will come up when I'm searching the Tube sites for something else. Sometimes, knowing everything I know, I'll still let them play. There are years of these scenes, decades' worth; once you watch one, the algorithm serves you ten more. The gestures are always the same, the sounds, the speed. The only thing that changes is his partners.

One Friday in early summer, everyone in the office piles into school buses so we can be taken to a mandatory party. It takes an hour to get to the beach the company has rented, which is actually a man-made lake somewhere half an hour outside the city.

I find the other poets. Together we eat charred veggie dogs and wait forty-five minutes in line to spend our drink tickets on cups of lukewarm beer, then sit down on the beach. All around us there are multiple kinds of EDM vibrating from different kinds of portable speakers our co-workers have brought from home. The IT expert jogs past me wearing a Hawaiian shirt; he seems to be genuinely enjoying himself, and his iPad is nowhere in sight. I feel a brief flash of pride in him, a misfiring impulse that may actually just be heatstroke.

After a few hours of marinating in the sun, we are all called into an enormous tent to watch our CEO give a speech. He announces that the company is having an amazing year, and to thank us all for our service they'll be implementing something called "summer Fridays," where everyone can leave the office an hour early in the warmer months. A cheer rises up from the crowd, until he clarifies that he means we will start doing this *next year.* The cheer dies down. When his speech is over, our CEO heads off with the other members of upper management to throw expensive items off a lifeguard tower as prizes for a dance contest.

The poets and I go to lie down on the reclining chairs that have been set up along the shore. It is pretty chill until a Frisbee comes flying at me, knocking my beer out of my hand and all down the front of my sundress. I tell everyone I'm going for a walk.

Farther down the beach, someone has haphazardly piled up a bunch of kayaks, paddles and life jackets. I pick out one of each that seems like it could be my size, drag the boat into the water and paddle steadily, out to the middle of the man-made lake. I stay out there for a while, facing away from the beach, floating in the man-made waves, watching the glittering pattern the sun makes on the water. *I'm completely and totally alone*, I think, but of course, it isn't true.

One morning before work I am sitting at my kitchen table, eating breakfast and staring at a pen embossed with the company logo, the giant stylized *M*. I keep this pen on the table for casual note-taking, and my gaze often lands on it while I am finishing my cereal and listening to the radio. I have probably spent hours staring at it while thinking about other things, not really noticing. But on this morning, all of a sudden, the logo on the pen rearranges itself. It is like looking at a Magic Eye poster and suddenly seeing the hidden image; a riddle unlocking. *The M looks like a pair of open legs.* It seems so jarringly obvious that I can't believe I didn't notice it before. It's not explicit, just a hint of a suggestion inside the image. But it's there. I think it's there. I'm pretty sure. The longer I stare at it, the less I can tell.

Later that afternoon, in the office, I emerge from a ten-minute bathroom break and realize the entire floor is empty. Everyone has disappeared from the office, but their glowing monitors indicate they only recently left. I can't help thinking of those Christian books about the Rapture where all the sinners get stuck on earth while the good, God-fearing people disappear, yanked up to heaven. A security guard appears in the doorway and tells me the office is being evacuated. *How come?* I ask. He shrugs and points toward the stairs.

People from higher floors are crowding into the stairwell, shuffling down to the ground floor at a pace that does not feel particularly urgent. I hear someone say *bomb threat* and think of what the IT expert said to me that first day in the elevator— how *this business used to be different.* When we exit the building, someone tells us to find our "teams" in the parking lot and stay with them. I weave my way through the crowd, trying to remember what any of my co-workers look like. Finally I recognize someone—a coder who comes to work every day in a black leather trench coat, no matter what the weather's like. I wander over to him and we nod at each other. I wonder whether he knows we work together. People keep streaming out of the building. The coder lights a cigarette while I hop up onto a concrete curb, trying to balance on one foot at a time. We survey the parking lot, which is beginning to crowd.

Eventually, he exhales a plume of smoke and shakes his head, jutting his chin toward the office. *What a sausagefest,* he says.

Do you think I'll get in trouble if I just go home? I ask.

Probably not, he says. So I do.

The next day, my father's wife calls me at lunchtime while I'm wandering through the cemetery. She works on a TV show where the writers' assistant has just quit at a crucial moment. They need to find a replacement for her before the season begins next week—someone who can take notes and organize everyone's script binders and hates their current job so much they'd be willing to leave it immediately. I was the first person who came to mind. Within forty-eight hours I have quit the porn company, sublet my apartment, and bought a bus ticket back home.

The TV show is about a doctor who is also a kind of ghost. More specifically he is in a coma, and as his physical form lies in the hospital his spirit wanders the halls, helping others in liminal states cross over into the next life or return to their bodies.

The writer's room occupies one wing of the enormous, industrial building where the show is filmed. The set where they film it is on the opposite end: a whole fake hospital filled with fake equipment, fake patients, fake machines blinking and beeping. The stories written on our side travel across the building, where they are received, interpreted and filmed. A clean exchange.

A few of the writers are in their twenties and thirties, but most of the staff are older. Many of them began their careers as playwrights, poets and fiction writers, until someone offered them a job writing for TV. Now they work in the industry full-time, own beautiful homes filled with beautiful children and beautiful dogs. *Television is the only place you can make real money as a writer*, they all say to me, repeatedly.

Eighty percent of my job is taking notes. I am good enough at it that after a few weeks, I can feel the younger writers' resentment at the nepotism that got me here beginning to dissolve. TV writing is a process unlike anything I have ever seen before: a mixture of group therapy, boardroom meeting and seance. I love taking notes during these sessions; it's fascinating to track the way an idea becomes a story through conversation, watching every individual thought get rock-tumbled through the collective mind of the group. I have never thought of writing as something you could do with other people. In this model, everyone feels responsible for the final product. No one has to carry it alone.

I have never had an interesting job before. I love it. I love the pale rainbow of the script pages in their binders. I love keeping track of everyone's schedules. I love the structure of an hour-long drama, the emotional unit of the beat. I love stocking the mini fridge with seltzer, making sure there are enough index cards in every colour. I love running to the corner with a muffin and a coffee every morning to meet the carpool. I love coming home at the end of the day exhausted, condensing the day's notes as fast as I can and sending them to everyone, maybe meeting a friend for a beer in the park for an hour or two before I'm too tired and have to come home. I love the deep, dreamless sleep I fall into at the end of the day, and I love getting up at 7:00 a.m. to do it all over again. I love the money I make and how little free time I have to spend it. I love the purpose and the structure, the pleasurable surrender of my life.

One afternoon there is a storm warning. Halfway through the afternoon, it starts to rain so intensely that everyone in the writer's room is sent home early. In the parking lot people wave goodbye to each other as they unlock their car doors, laughing nervously. The sky is slate grey, the air flashing lavender.

I ride home with the two youngest women on staff, the script supervisor and the story coordinator, who is the only one of the three of us who owns a car. The rain is so thick we can barely see through the windshield. People are stopped in the middle of the road—tires spinning in the water, making waves until they sputter out.

We get on the highway that leads back into the city. It is completely empty, not a single other car. Later we will learn that they closed this road to drivers nearly an hour before we got on, and we should never have been able to drive on it—someone must have forgotten to close off our on-ramp. The story coordinator is a very cautious driver; we move at a safe and steady pace, and everything is fine until we hit a deep puddle and nearly hydroplane into the median. The story coordinator's favourite band is U2, and because she is driving, we are listening to them very loudly on the stereo. My first thought when we hit the water is *I wonder whether "Vertigo" will be the last song I hear before I die.* Somehow the car finds traction at the last second, and after that we are all flooded with adrenaline, our breathing sharp and audible, filling the car. My pulse pumps glitter through my body.

When we get back into town, it's beautiful. The water covering the ground creates a twin city below us, like driving on top of a mirror. Everything's doubled and shimmering: the sparkling lights of backed-up traffic, the purple sky, people rushing home with their useless umbrellas turned inside out. When we pull up to my apartment it is like getting out of a gondola in Venice. I soak my ankles in the tide lapping against the curb.

When I go to sleep it's still raining. But when I wake up the next morning, the sky is clear and the streets are dry. The story coordinator picks me up at the usual corner outside the usual café in her car, and we spend the drive talking about work. Once we arrive, no one really has time to talk about what happened the night before. If it weren't for the machines sucking water up loudly from the carpets, you'd never know anything happened at all.

On the weekend I go to a reading. In a corner near the bathroom, I run into the editor of the Books section of a local newspaper. He is talking to one of the editors from the small press I interned at, summers ago. I chat with them for a while, and the Books editor asks if I'd ever be interested in writing reviews of other people's novels. He says he keeps a list of potential reviewers and if I'd like to be put on it I should send him an email. I say *Yeah for sure absolutely* without really thinking about it.

And don't forget—when you finish your first book, we have first dibs! the small-press editor says, smiling. She is just being friendly, I know that—I'm not sure she's ever read a single thing I've written—but something about the statement startles me out of my half-attentive daze. My spine vibrates like a struck tuning fork. I excuse myself and walk away, shaking, like I've gotten away with something.

The writers are working on an episode where someone gets hit by lightning and lives. I schedule a call with a doctor who can give the staff a lecture about what happens to the body in this situation. We crowd into someone's quiet, dark office, hit the speakerphone button and lean toward the receiver. *There's a pattern that spiderwebs across your skin*, he explains, *like a tattoo.* This mark is always exactly the same shape and pattern as the actual bolt that struck you in the first place. *Over in 1/100ᵗʰ of a second*, say my notes, *but it lives on your body forever.*

In the middle of a very busy day I get a phone call. It is some-one from the government, telling me I've been awarded a grant I applied for almost a year ago. I am going to attend a studio residency at the country's most prestigious artist's centre for seven whole weeks. They ask me when I want to go. I pick a date next spring, forever away. Then I say thank you, hang up, and go back to work.

The season ends. I use my last month's pay to buy a new laptop and hire two men to move all my belongings from my old apartment in my old city to here. I put down first and last months' rent on a new apartment—a one-bedroom, so the musician and I can move in together. Then the TV money's gone, like I never had it at all.

THREE

The conversation always takes the same shape, though the content varies. We've honed the structure through years of trial and error, reflection, affirmation.

First we talk about the movie. Each time I am newly astounded at how the three of us can sit together in the same room, watching the same footage for hours, and come away with completely different impressions of what we saw and what it meant. The times when we agree feel like magic.

Eventually we turn toward our lives. One by one, we take turns describing the major events of the week, everything that's happened since the last time we met. While one person speaks, the other two watch her the same way we watched the movie. Sometimes our interpretations match, and sometimes they diverge. We match the things that happened this week to things like them that happened weeks before. We illuminate their common themes, make sense of ourselves for each other. It is a privilege to have your life witnessed like this, with such care and attention. To have the scattered points of you arranged into a line.

The Craigslist post says the SEO company is looking for a *high-powered content creator*. I don't actually know what an SEO is, but I reply with my resume anyway. Within a few hours someone writes me back, saying they think I could be a great fit. *These people must be desperate*, I think, as I schedule the interview.

When I arrive at their office, it's a house. I stand on the curb, shifting back and forth from my heels to my toes, and pull out my phone to check the address. I have it right. *Did they ever say "office"?* I scroll back through the email chain. There is no phone number for me to call.

Okay, I say to myself, scrambling to recalibrate. *It's probably fine.* I knock too hard on the door, trying to arrange my face in a neutral position. When a young guy answers I hesitate, scanning for any obvious signs that he plans to murder me. He's a white man in his late twenties, with heavy eyelids and hair that makes it seem like he either just got out of bed or is making a deliberate choice to look that way. It is impossible to tell. He invites me inside. While I'm still deciding what to do, I enter.

The house is open-plan, messy and creepily silent. Multiple gaming consoles hum and glow along the far wall of the living room. A large flatscreen TV is bolted to the wall above them, hospital-style. In between the living room and kitchen areas there is a large, round, heavy glass kitchen table that looks like it may once have been patio furniture. The kitchen's black marble countertops are littered with blender bottles and open containers of protein powder. An item that I think might be a chin-up bar hangs in the doorway that leads to the rest of the house.

I'm not sure whether to take my shoes off. Before I get the chance to ask, the guy who answered the door invites another, taller version of himself into the room. With an uncannily synchronized gesture they invite me to sit down, and begin explaining their business.

The two men are brothers. They started this company together a few years ago but it's still getting off the ground— *Hence the home office*, they say with a wry, simultaneous grin. But it's been growing, and now they need a copywriter. *There's a lot of stuff we just can't afford to keep doing ourselves*, says the older brother, who looks like a refrigerator with a face drawn on it. He handles *the big picture stuff*, he explains. The younger one of him will be my manager.

After about thirty more seconds of obligatory small talk, the older brother asks whether I think the job sounds good. *Yes*, I say, though I still don't understand anything about it. He stands up, goes *Okay, now my bro's going to show you the ropes*, and disappears. My new boss invites me into his office.

I should not be surprised that it's his bedroom, but I am. There's a large, unmade bed in the corner, covers twisted up like someone only recently got out. Most of the rest of the space is taken up by a large, L-shaped desk: big ugly monitors, comically oversized chair, and an ergonomic keyboard that looks like an acid-induced hallucination, splitting apart from itself. Against the wall at the end of the bed, there's a large bookshelf filled with video games. On the top sits an empty glass bottle shaped like a human skull.

I recognize this skull. It is the signature vessel of a brand of vodka produced by a C-list celebrity, the most famous person currently living (part-time) in the musician's hometown. A friend once gave us one of these bottles as an expensive joke, and now we keep it on top of our fridge. The skull is unsettling but also impossible to throw away. The one that looks down on me now, from my new manager's bedroom bookshelf, is wearing an enormous pair of Beats by Dre headphones. I know from reading the copy on the tag around the neck of the bottle that this vodka has been filtered multiple times through a type of quartz that is supposed to raise it to a higher level of vibration. For a second I try to imagine my new boss drinking high-vibration vodka out of a human skull, feeling its uncommon power sweeping through his body, cleansing him of impure energies. While I am doing this he scoots up next to me in his rolling chair, minimizes sixteen tabs on one of his monitors, and clears his throat. *Okay!* he says, in the tone of a real manager at a real office, and not a jock in his own dusty bedroom. *Let's get to work.*

The younger brother spends an hour explaining the mechanics of my new job. I try to take notes while he talks, but it's difficult. His language is specific enough that the work sounds legitimate, but vague enough that no matter how much he tells me, I still don't really understand what he's talking about.

SEO, the younger brother says, stands for "Search Engine Optimization." The company exists to help small business owners float their websites as close to the top of Google's search rankings as possible—so they can be the first site a person sees when they're searching for the products or services that business sells. My job will be to write blog posts for these clients. *Blog posts are very important,* he says. I write BLOG POSTS in all caps and underline it twice.

Once they've been written, the brothers send these blog posts to someone he describes as *a guy,* who maintains a constellation of blogs each based around a different overarching theme: skin care, home repair, fashion, etc. The more a client pays, the more I write, the more the post guy posts. The younger brother pulls up and scrolls through a few of these blogs, never resting long enough for me to actually read the text, though I can see that every paragraph is scattered with hyperlinks, all coloured and bolded and underlined. I recognize the layout of these sites—I have stumbled onto pages like them while trying to illegally download music or TV shows. They are the kinds of websites you click out of as fast as you possibly can.

Once a blog post goes up, the younger brother explains, the brothers send the link to what he calls *a team of people overseas.* These people are paid to click on the keyword links embedded in the post's text over and over. All this clicking inflates the number of hits that lead to the client's website, which in turn boosts their search engine rankings. This is, of course, if everything goes according to plan. The brothers do not sell a guarantee; they are simply in the business of improving their clients' odds. They do not, as far as I can tell, offer refunds.

After an hour of watching him scroll through websites and spreadsheets and tabs, the younger brother asks whether I have any questions. I ask whether I can use the bathroom, and he directs me to an en suite off his older brother's bedroom.

The bathroom is tiled in shiny, oppressive black. It's like peeing inside an expensively detailed sensory deprivation tank. Next to the toilet is a pile of SEO industry magazines. I flip through one of them and am shocked by how little of the terminology I understand: *Linked unstructured citations, amplification, domain authority, render-blocking scripts.* A whole other language, hidden inside the one I thought I knew.

=

At this point, the musician and I have been living together for two or three months. Our apartment is on a large, noisy street north of the subway, on the ground floor of a small two-story house that's been hastily divided in three. Our landlords are two cousins who look nearly identical but have very different functions: one of them does repairs, and the other collects our rent. They bought the place together and split it up as quickly as they could to maximize their income, so the ghost of the single-family home it used to be still haunts our apartment. Outside our bathroom you can see a sealed-off door to the basement. In our bedroom, behind the dresser, there's a boarded-up entrance that once led to the front hall.

Our place is objectively too small for two people obsessed with shopping at thrift stores. The collections of records, books, clothes and instruments that made each of our previous apartments feel expansive and interesting make this place cramped and claustrophobic, no matter how carefully we arrange them. Our living room is also our office and dining room; along every wall, there are shelves crammed full of stuff. A toy *Ghostbusters* proton pack, a smiling stuffed Garfield holding a novelty plastic lobster, a colourful string of glowing plastic parrot lights, three guitars (the 12-string doubleneck, the orange Flying V and the all-white vintage Stratocaster like the one Wayne lusts after in *Wayne's World,* with a sun-bleached vintage button that says TAKE OFF, HOSER on the strap), the covers of twelve different Prince albums strung up in a garland, an enormous *Star Trek* poster, a framed photo of me and my mother and my grandmother on a Mediterranean cruise from three years ago, a poster of a puppy and a kitten touching noses that says FRIENDS FOREVER underneath. On the wall above the couch, the musician has mounted a novelty licence plate that bears the phrase: ALL I *WANT* IS MORE THAN I EVER HAD. It's a souvenir he found on tour once, in a gas station somewhere between Georgia and South Carolina. The phrase made such an impression that it has worked its way into many of his songs— repeated over and over like a mantra. If you were to walk past our apartment and look in through the living room window, you'd see it floating above my head like a thought bubble.

All these objects do little to insulate us against our neighbours' lives. The walls and floors of the house are so thin that living there feels like being in an intimate relationship with everyone else in the building, separately and simultaneously. The woman who lives below us is a makeup artist who gets up each day at 5:00 a.m. and complains daily to her long-distance boyfriend about my boyfriend's guitar noodling. The couple who live above us own a pet bird, hate each other, and are half-way through twin master's degrees in film studies. I fall asleep to the soundtracks of the movies they watch and wake up to the sound of their arguing.

Working from home means that on weekday mornings I bolt out of bed as late as I possibly can, scarf down my break-fast, bring my laptop over to our bright yellow Formica kitchen table or our wet-sand-coloured couch, and sign in. The brothers insist we do all our communication through Skype chat. I type *hello* so they can tell I'm at my computer, and then they give me my assignments for the day.

I am the first and only full-time employee the brothers have ever hired. It's a gamble they are hoping will pay off. Other people in their industry farm out the task of copywriting to websites with names like Textbroker, where contractors bid on the right to write 500-word blog posts for five dollars apiece. The text that surrounds the hyperlinks in each blog post is incidental, not really meant to be read, let alone scrutinized.

But search engines do not like when people try to game their systems. As the brothers explain it to me, they have an army of robots trawling the internet, searching for content designed to game their system. If they detect too much repetition in a blog post it's flagged, and the sites it links to are pulled down in the rankings. Likewise, if a post seems not to have been written by a human at all—too many grammatical fractures, spelling errors, tangled sentences—it's immediately under suspicion.

The brothers have decided the best way to get past these bots is by using a real writer. My job is to sound as much like a real human being as I possibly can without doing any of the real human things that might strip away the content's calibrated optimization: no non-sequiturs, no unexpected turns of phrase, no unnecessary off-topic information, no mentioning competing brands or products. Nothing too interesting or boring, too like or unlike anything else.

As the weeks unspool, I develop a strange, piecemeal intimacy with the younger brother, who drops stray details from his personal life into the chat in moments I never expect them. I learn that the brothers are both very interested in the band Phish, but between the two of them the older one is the real diehard. They recently built a studio with a floating floor and perfect acoustics in the basement, so they can go down there and jam to let off steam at the end of a tough workday.

One afternoon, when I am typing away, the chat pings. The younger brother wants to know if I've ever played competitive dodgeball. His team, he explains, needs *at least one chick* to qualify for league play; right now they're short. I wonder whether this is some kind of test, or whether it is actually true that he knows so few women he needs to ask an employee he's only met once to join his team. For a second, I let myself think about what it might be like to be the lone chick on my imaginary boss's amateur competitive sports team, sweating it out with him in the paint, both of us fixed on the goal of whipping another co-ed group with soft foam balls.

Sorry, I type, after a long pause. *I'm not very good at sports.* There is no response. Eventually I notice he has gone offline.

I write for a wide and bizarre range of clients: gardeners, hair-stylists, people who make laptop skins and "urban socks." I write about how much I love getting facial peels at the best Toronto spas, about my painful longing for a contractor who can skilfully waterproof my basement.

No matter how much I write, some of these businesses remain incomprehensible to me. It's a bit like how it's possible to watch an entire movie about a sports team and understand the narrative arc of the story without ever learning the actual rules of the game. I do not know what concrete resurfacing is, but I can tell you all about the benefits of getting it done to your driveway. I know all the reasons to take a "helicopter skiing vacation," because we have two separate clients who do nothing but plan and execute them, but I absolutely cannot tell you what they involve. Do they drop you *out of a helicopter*? Or do they take you up to the top of the mountain in a helicopter and then let you out in a place where you put on your skis and *then* ski down? I will never know the answer, no matter how many times I type that it's the most thrilling winter vacation money can buy.

One of the greatest new challenges is figuring out how to bend the grammar of these posts around the ideas they're meant to convey, like light moving around a fixed object. One of the most common keyword phrases I'm supposed to insert into the text is *best [whatever] Toronto*, because it's a common search phrase: *best boxing Toronto, best juice Toronto, best lunch Toronto*. This is not how anyone actually talks, even if it's how they search; trying to work it into a sentence is endlessly frus-trating, and I have to do it dozens of times a day.

Eventually, I come up with a genius solution, a way to make the phrase elegant and seamless: *These are some of the* best sandwiches Toronto *has to offer! This boxing class is the* best boxing class Toronto *has seen in some time!* I am inordinately proud of myself for this trick. I feel a distant, hollow echo of the triumphant pride that comes from writing a good poem, when I find a way to turn pages of sprawling idea into a single line.

Of course, no one ever acknowledges my innovation. And just like with art, the rush of a breakthrough inevitably gives way to self-doubt. My inability to come up with other equally elegant constructions begins to haunt me, and as time passes I worry I've peaked early, feel genuine anxiety about my inability to follow up my one true achievement with anything that compares to its genius.

I hide most of my keywords and links at the end of each post, inside a false biography of the post's imaginary author. Bios are the best place to put everything, the younger brother tells me, because the bots don't scan them as carefully as the text. Each bio is structured the same way. I get to choose my own pseudonym, then I browse through some copyright-free stock photos to find a new picture for myself. Today, for example, I am Alison, a thin, toned blonde woman in jogging gear. I am standing alone in a beautiful, empty field, gazing with a strong sense of vague purpose out into the middle distance. The sun is rising or setting behind me; either way, light filters through my high ponytail. I look hopeful and proud.

Alison is a wannabe yogi, social media guru, and mother of two who loves to share her exciting discoveries about the Toronto roofing *industry online!* I type, staring into my own pixelated eyes as I gaze off into the new or dying day.

I like this part of the job, the first-person-ness. It's fun, trying to inhabit the mind of a fictional person who might be enough of a luxury watch enthusiast or Botox addict to write a string of enthusiastic posts on the topic. I covet expensive things and dream about splurging on elaborate luxury vacations, I worry that the effects of time will one day render me hideous. My desires and fears are pure, and so are my intentions. I just want to tell you about this amazing deal I've found on something that is going to fix all of your problems forever.

One morning, a few months in, the younger brother sends me a message: *Big changes going down today.* The search engine has recalibrated the algorithm they use to monitor and evaluate content. Our current format will no longer fly, he tells me; no more opinions or recommendations or biographies, no more first-person narration. We need to start working with facts, or at least writing in a way that conveys a convincingly fact-like impression.

These new posts are incredibly boring to write. I put them together the same way I used to write book reports in the fifth grade: an hour or so before they're due, I skim the Wikipedia page for a topic related to the service the client offers, and then I rearticulate a few stock facts in a vaguely authoritative, omniscient tone. I methodically weed out flourishes, jokes, any semblance of structure that isn't straightforward. Value judgements and tone—the features that used to make a first-person blog post convincing—now drag against the nature of the text:

> Botox procedures involve safely injecting a chemical formula into the body. The effects of Botox can last anywhere from three to six months. Botox can be used to treat a number of medical conditions, such as hyperhidrosis and migraine headaches, in addition to reversing the effects of aging.

One of the brothers' biggest clients is a company called SKIN ENERGY, with the name in all caps like that, every time. Many of the small businesses I write for will disappear from my memory the second I leave this job, but SKIN ENERGY will stay lodged in my mind until I die, burned in like a bright image that's been projected on the same screen for too long.

SKIN ENERGY is a Botox clinic, and they order more posts than any of the brothers' other clients. They are serious about the content of their fake blog posts; the CEO reviews them personally, and frequently emails the brothers when he sees something in my work he doesn't like. I spend about 60 percent of my time writing for and about them.

On SKIN ENERGY days I write anywhere from five to twenty posts at once. I come up with a system to manage the tedium: I write the titles of the posts first, setting a timer for three minutes and spitting out as many as I can in a fevered, dissociative rush. I work like someone speaking in tongues, taken over by the spirit of Optimization itself. When the alarm rings, I sit back and look at what I've done. Then I spend the rest of the day working backward, writing posts to fit the titles:

+ Your guide to turning back the hands of time with Botox!
+ Is aging skin affecting your mood? Botox can be the answer!
+ Need relief from wrinkles? Botox clinics can give you what you need!
+ Getting older can be devastating, but Botox can help!
+ Concerned about crow's feet? Botox is your secret weapon!

The thesis of all these posts is that it doesn't matter whether you spend your life laughing or crying—the longer you live, the more you feel, and the uglier you get because of it. Even happiness leaves its mark on you forever, and that mark will eventually make you impossible to love. *Time comes for everyone*, I type, hunched forward and frowning. *But thankfully, there's a solution!*

Time turns liquid inside the constraints of this job. An hour can have anything in it. I am paid according to the assumption that I will sit at my computer from nine to five every day, Monday to Friday, with small breaks for lunch or going to the bathroom. I quickly discover I do not need eight hours a day to do my job competently. Everything takes exactly as long as I give myself to do it. If I decide I only have one hour, I can compress a day's worth of work down into those sixty minutes. I am like one of those industrial crushers that can turn a whole car into a single metal cube.

When I'm not working I pace the apartment, reheat leftovers, scroll through Twitter, feeling a faint buzz in the back of my skull. I dust the shelves. I change my clothes. I flip through the musician's record collection, shopping for a mood. I walk the same four-block circle around our place, greeting the neighbourhood cats. I become briefly, feverishly obsessed with the reality show *Catfish: The TV Show*, and then with a reality show called *Dating Naked*, and then a reality show called *Love Prison*, which I am almost certainly the only person to have seen all of without being directly involved in its production.

Sometimes I write book reviews for the newspaper. The work gives me a sturdy, functional kind of pleasure. I read each book I am assigned with dutiful attention to detail, flagging important passages with Post-it notes. I research the authors' back catalogues. I try to describe each book as accurately as I can, and maybe offer a little assessment of whether the text is doing what its author seems to want it to do, if I have space. Writing for the newspaper is like writing a formal poem, or a fake blog post. The form dictates the content, more or less.

Sometimes, if I really need to escape, I type *hey just heading out for lunch* into the chat and then walk all the way to a large mall over half an hour from my house. I know I will theoretically be in trouble if the brothers try to chat with me and I don't respond, but I don't actually know how "being in trouble" at this job would work, or what the potential repercussions could possibly be. I don't usually buy anything at the mall. I just wander around the stores in a glassy daze, appreciating how much of everything there is, the meticulous organization of every store.

Sometimes, when I'm walking around touching T-shirts, I'll think about my novel, the one I failed to finish in university. I have not actually worked on it since the porn office, but lately I've been revising the plot in my mind. Instead of being about a young, smart, fascinating teenage girl, the story is now about a quietly attractive, secretly brilliant young woman in her mid-twenties who works at a porn office and lives in a city that is slowly being swallowed by a massive sinkhole that grows larger with each passing day.

Our protagonist works as a video editor, but her truest desire is to become a film artist. One day, a co-worker tells her about a production company—a small subsidiary of the one they work for—that takes porn scripts written on spec. There's an email address to which you can send your scenes, and if someone ends up shooting them, they'll direct-deposit $250 into your bank account.

Something about this idea appeals to the protagonist. At first, she writes scenes on her lunch break; just generic porn shit, *hospital, stepmom,* whatever. The scenes are quick to write; you only need to do the beginning and the end. After a month or two of submitting her work into the void, she finally sees a deposit land in her bank account. When she types a few relevant phrases into the search bar of the enormous porn website and sorts by Newest First, her scene is there. It is bizarre to hear her words in the mouths of these performers, as the placeholder texts they are for some reason required to say out loud before they can start fucking. After submitting a few scenes and watching them play out this way, she begins to send in work that is more specifically based on her life—an online dating interaction, or a strange moment at the grocery store. A weird dentist's appointment, or the long bathroom breaks she spends just killing time at work.

Her scenes are popular. The more she writes, the more get made. And the longer she does it, the closer each scene gets to reality. She starts copying dialogue from her own conversations, gives her characters the names of her friends and family members. She watches performers act out conversations she's had with her best friends, watches them speak her most private sentiments and fears out loud. What she's doing feels thrilling and terrifying. She feels like maybe she should stop, but she can't. She knows she's doing something incredibly stupid, perverted, morally wrong. Or maybe she's making art.

Evening, late winter. The musician and I are cooking dinner with the radio on, and the DJ plays the Bruce Springsteen song "I'm Goin' Down." The musician says, absentmindedly, *This is such an amazing song about that horrible feeling just before you break up with someone. The thing where you know it's going to happen, but it hasn't happened yet. Do you know what I mean?*

No, I say, so fast and hard it snuffs the conversation out.

There is definitely something wrong with our relationship, but since I can't figure out what it is, I've decided it's probably me. I try cleaning the house more and not cleaning the house so much. I try talking more, then less, about my feelings. I try meditation and running and journaling and stretching and mindfulness. I quit caffeine. I start caffeine again. I up the dosage of my antidepressants and add another pill. I go to therapy. And as a last-ditch effort, I decide to get an MFA in creative writing from an American university.

I've been having different versions of this idea for years. In high school, I wanted to go to an American college because I'd spent my life watching American television and reading American books and listening to American music, and it seemed like the place where all serious artists went to become themselves. In university, I often heard real writers giving speeches in bars about why most Canadian books were so terrible. The abundance of arts grants in Canada, they told each other, had made the country a place where mediocre art flourished and reproduced like mould. Canada, these writers all agreed, lacked a sense of urgency, a competitive edge. In America there were no government-sponsored grants, and the lack of resources available to artists made them fiercely competitive. In America, only the strong survived.

Some parts of this argument made sense to me. A lot of the most commercially successful Canadian books I'd read *were* pretty bad, and many of their authors were white, middle-aged men who seemed to write because it was their job, not because they had anything interesting to say. But the men at the bar who railed against the mediocrity of their industry never complained about whiteness or maleness. They never ranted about the systemic racism built into a publishing industry historically unwilling to give a platform to anyone who wasn't white. They never railed against colonialism or transphobia or ableism or even plain old misogyny. Their frustration with "Canadian literature" always turned out to be professional jealousy dressed up as righteous indignation: they were mad at the industry not because it had failed so many others, but because it had failed to recognize *them*.

Usually, if I could sense one of these speeches coming on, I'd take it as my cue to go get another drink. But something about all that ranting must have struck a chord in me, because whenever I found myself frustrated with my experiences at university, I'd think wistfully about what my life would be like if I'd gone to school in America instead. Maybe, in a country where everything was two hundred times more expensive and a thousand times more exclusive, people might take their jobs more seriously. Maybe the professors in prestigious American creative writing programs wouldn't hold their lectures in bars, or teach hungover, or use their classrooms as dating pools, because they took their responsibilities seriously. Maybe, in a country where it was nearly impossible to make art, it might mean something to want to learn.

I join an online forum for prospective MFA applicants and read every single post twice. I spend hours taking studious notes on the pros and cons of every school that offers a full scholarship. I take the GRE with a friend, a poet with dual citizenship who can't decide whether she wants to quit writing or devote her life to it. The exam takes place in a sweaty, tiny room in a building uptown crammed with nervous, silent people who do not look at each other. I do poorly on every section but English. For weeks after, I have generic, humiliating high-school nightmares—forgetting my locker combination, failing the math test that turns to water in my hands.

I write to the schools and ask them to waive my application fees, because I cannot afford them on my SEO paycheque. I write sheepish notes to old professors asking for letters of recommendation, and grovelling follow-up requests when they forget. I bookmark the financial aid pages for each school and reread them until my eyes glaze over. The tuition numbers are so high they seem fictional. *You can't put a price on America*, I tell the musician, my friends, my family. Everyone nods. I know they are humouring me, but I actually think I might be right. The fact is, you get paid more to write in America, whether it's an essay or a book, and you can't access that money unless you've been there, met the right people and convinced them of your worth. I have already seen how much success in the arts depends on knowing people who can help you, on making your name into one that people have already heard.

I make it onto two waiting lists, and then I wait. When one of the schools eventually offers me a spot, the letter is addressed to a "Mr. Healey," with the *r* scratched out and replaced with an *s* in blue ballpoint. I show the letter to my mother and she congratulates me. I show the letter to the musician and he congratulates me. No one wants to tell me what to do.

Later that night, the musician and I decide to watch the first episode of a new and very popular TV show. It's one of those detective stories where two very serious men chase down a mystery that only grows deeper as they pursue it, each new detail sending them further into a question that will never completely resolve.

The show, coincidentally, is set in the same state as the school that has just accepted me. The opening shot of the first episode is of a dead, naked woman lashed to a tree. The killer has placed an animal skull over her head. We both laugh a little, nervously. *America!* I say. I keep saying it over and over. Before we go to bed, I check the school's tuition page again. Then I throw the acceptance letter away.

A few weeks later, chatting with my manager, we somehow end up on the subject of tests. I mention that I recently did poorly on the GRE and he says he can sympathize. I ask whether he ever had to take it, and he tells me he went to school in the States. *I studied electroacoustics*, he says. I don't know what that is, but I'm impressed.

It turns out the younger brother has an expensive arts degree from a prestigious American college. He lived in New York City for years, he tells me, and he loved it there. He only moved back to Toronto because he ran out of money and his visa was expiring. His brother wanted to start a business, and it just seemed like the smart thing to do. He really loves synthesizers, he tells me, and he misses getting to mess with them all day. He misses the city, misses making music with his friends. *But in the end*, he types, *you can't make a living doing that kind of stuff.*

In the spring, the brothers let me take two months off for my residency at the Centre for the Arts.

The Centre is built on top of a mountain in a rich town in a rich province that has made most of its money through the procurement and extraction of oil and gas from the earth. The facility has two main functions: to provide space and time for artists to focus on their work, and to provide space and time for corporations that need somewhere to hold conferences. The meeting rooms and the art studios are located on different parts of the campus, but everyone shares the rest. In the dining hall, some tables have little reservation cards on them that just say ARTISTS, so neither group is accidentally forced to interact with the other over meals.

By the time you get there, you've already paid for everything. Caretakers turn down your bed, clean your room, prepare your meals and give you clean towels at the gym, which you don't even have to go outside to get to. On top of a mountain, away from your day job and your family and your chores and your concerns, you can finally be an artist and nothing else.

On my first day, after I drop off my stuff in my room and am given instructions about what to do if I am attacked by a bear while out for a beautiful walk in the picturesque mountains, I pick up the keys to my studio. To get there, I have to duck off the main road that runs from the campus down the mountain and cross a little bridge into a patch of trees. It's like stepping into a secret world, an enchanted fairy-tale forest. Sun filters down through dense clusters of pine trees, throwing patterned shade all over. It is the quietest place I have ever been.

Each studio in the forest is designed by a different architect, intended for a different kind of artist. My studio, the writer's studio, is a refurbished boat. It is shockingly beautiful from the outside—majestic and surreal to see in the middle of the woods, adrift in a sea of pine needles. Inside, it's like a fancy RV. There's a desk running along the stern, with a large computer set under a porthole window. In the bow there's a kitchen with a kettle and a tiny couch for napping. In the cutlery drawer I find two forks, a wine opener and a guestbook, where residents are supposed to sign their names and leave a little message for posterity. I scan down the list of signatures, looking for famous names.

Once I've unpacked my bags and arranged all my pens, I sit down at the desk. Through the porthole, I can see the winter's last patches of snow melting on the forest floor. A pickup truck-sized elk wanders into view, and I feel my breath catch; even though we're separated by the walls of the boat, it is the closest I've ever been to an animal this size outside a zoo. The elk circles the boat a few times, then lies down beneath the window so all I can see is the sunlight tangling in its antlers.

Finally, I am alone. There is nothing else I can distract myself with. I turn on the computer. My plan is to begin this new draft of the novel from scratch—free of all my old, clunky ideas about how it should sound or what it should be. I open up a fresh new document. I put my hands on the keyboard, wrists arched like a concert pianist's, and wait for my novel to flow through me.

I keep waiting for a while, and then I check my email, and then I check every social media platform a few times. I send a few texts to the musician and my friends, showing them pictures of the boat and of the forest. After a few hours, I decide that maybe starting from scratch isn't the best idea. I plug in a USB key, click open an old draft of the novel, and start scrolling through the whole thing—something I have not actually done in over a year.

By the time I finish reading, I know beyond a shadow of a doubt that I am absolutely fucked. There is nothing there, really; just the things I wrote in high school and the scattered attempts I made at returning to the idea all through university. Most pages end mid-paragraph, mid-sentence, and are never picked up. The whole thing is less than fifty pages long. A real novel has a clear vision behind it: it has rising action, a sparkling cast, a sweeping voice, a hero's journey. All I've done is write the same scene again and again, with minor variations: a woman standing next to a black hole, watching it swallow the world.

At night, I eat dinner with the other writers. There is a separate literary program running at the Centre, and on its first night I walked past them: a group of maybe twenty people, various ages, gathered at the bar. I recognized one woman from the city—she's a poet, a friend of friends whose birthday party I once crashed—and she invited me to join their group. She has come to the Centre to work on a novel about a woman who is in love with a bridge. *Objectumsexual* is the term, she tells me, handing me a drink.

I am grateful for the presence of the other writers; it feels like we're sharing something, even though our experiences of staying at the Centre are fundamentally different. The grant that pays for my time at the Centre covers my food, lodging and studio fees, plus the costs of a return trip; I haven't had to give up anything to be here. But the other writers have paid tuition: thousands of dollars each for a three-week program. Their time here costs a lot of money, and each passing day brings with it increasing pressure to justify the expense.

Every evening at dinner, the group performs a ritual. This practice is as essential a component of residency at the Centre as complaining about the cafeteria food or giving the elk a wide berth when they pass you. No one ever talks about it directly— there is no collective decision or agreement to participate. It happens exactly the same way each time. Everybody just knows what to do.

It starts with one person asking another how their day was. The answering writer either says *I actually got some stuff done* or *It was so terrible I completely wasted the day and I feel like shit.* If they had a genuinely productive day, they speak with the glowing smugness of a person who is having secret, thrilling sex with a brand new partner. If they failed to produce, they talk about themselves like *Can you believe this fucking idiot?* Then everyone else at the table offers their sympathies or their congratulations, depending on the circumstances.

No one really likes hearing about a good day, but someone who's feeling generous will always politely go, *That's great, good for you.* A bad day is much easier to talk about. Everyone's self-flagellating self-talk is the same: *fake, pointless, wasting time, wasting money, not getting anywhere,* etc. I like hearing other writers talk like this—not because I like people being unkind to themselves, but because it's comforting to know I'm not the only one who does it so aggressively. Eventually the day-haver asks someone else down the table how *their* day was, and they answer, and so on, again and again.

After some trial and error, I develop the routine I will follow for most of my seven-week stay. I am not good at morning conversation, so to avoid the chance of having to engage in it, I spend my mornings in the gym, jogging half-heartedly on the treadmill until just before the breakfast buffet shuts down. Then I run upstairs, scarf down an enormous plate of eggs, and spend the rest of the morning wandering around the mountain until it's time for lunch. When I can't put it off any longer, I trudge into the boat and spend my afternoon staring at the screen, contemplating all the things I am failing to accomplish.

One morning, while I'm eating breakfast, something strange happens. I like to take a table against one of the enormous windows that line one whole wall of the room, offering a view of the mountains so cinematically gorgeous it seems fake. I am sitting in such a way that I can see all the way across the room. On the other end, across a sea of empty tables, I see a semi-familiar shape. I try to look closer without craning my neck. It looks kind of like the critically acclaimed, award-winning novelist who taught the last fiction workshop I ever took, making his way through a plate of waffles and eggs.

At first, I am completely unsurprised to see him here. The pull of my failure to write this novel feels so strong that his appearance seems weirdly inevitable, like I conjured him into the Centre with the sheer force of my will. It is only after I give myself a little time to think this through that I realize it makes no actual sense.

Then I realize he's looking at me. We make brief eye contact and he raises his eyebrows a little. Suddenly I am a trapped animal against the glass. I can sense the mountains looming behind me, all the muscles in my body locking in place. Instead of returning his gaze, I look down. I keep my eyes on my plate until twenty minutes later, when one of the waitstaff comes over and asks me to leave. *We have to start setting up for lunch,* he says. When I look up, the writer's table is empty. I wonder whether he was ever there at all.

The program holds a mixer for residents and the literary faculty who are here to mentor them. My poet friend asks me if I want to go and I say yes, because I want to see what she's like at a professional function, and also because I am becoming obsessed with her; she has a sharp, dry sense of humour that frightens dull men but pulls women toward her like a magnet. Plus there's supposed to be free wine.

The mixer reminds me of the awards ceremonies I used to visit in the creative writing program; the same thick-stemmed wine glasses, the same little cubes of cheese and trays of dry crudités. I suppress the urge to shove a handful of carrot sticks into my purse. Everything is so exactly like I remember it that when I see my former professor across the room, once again, it makes perfect sense.

I make small talk with whomever, nervously refilling my wine glass with tepid, sweet Chardonnay. Despite my strenuous avoidance, after a while the professor comes toward me. I want nothing more than to turn into a fine mist that will float out of my corporeal form and settle in a nice air duct somewhere above the room. Instead I turn around, smile, and say *Hello!* in a voice two octaves higher than my own.

We make polite small talk for a while. I explain that I'm not really in the literary program, that I'm here on a grant. When he asks what I'm working on, I tell him I'm finishing a novel, and he nods.

You were always a talented writer, he says. He asks whether I ever did anything with that story, *the one about the girl who ate the radio. Did you publish it anywhere? I remember it was so unique, so interesting. Really a lot of potential.*

This is more focused and specific commentary on my work than he ever offered when he was being paid to read it. I wonder if it is possible that he actually remembers that story. An image flashes into my mind, unbidden, of this man sitting at his laptop, searching through his old emails for my name. I shake my head to clear it. *Don't be crazy.*

A day or two after the party, a message pops up in my inbox. The professor wants to know whether I would like to meet up and talk about literature sometime. He says that we can sit under a tree, that he knows a place in town where he can get a nice bottle of French wine.

This message is like a poem—there are the words, and then there is a second universe of meaning hidden inside them, something I can sense without being able to name. Reading it sets off a sour churning in my stomach.

I call the musician and tell him about it. *Gross*, he says. I ask my new poet friend to read it and she wrinkles her nose. *Fuck this guy*, she says. Later, at the bar with a group of women, I pass my phone around so they can see it. *Oh god*, says everyone. Then we start telling our stories.

As their time at the Centre runs out, I watch the other writers' moods decline. In the beginning, almost everyone was awed at how much work they were able to accomplish in a day with no family or day job or chores or errands or children. There was a shared sense of openness, possibility, *relief.*

But as the days start to dwindle, the fantasy feeling gives way to a crushing sense of pressure. Everyone worries they haven't made the most of their experience. They have fallen short of the goals they promised themselves they'd achieve, or they got something done but it wasn't the right thing. They worry that they have not made enough art, or enough good art, or enough perfect art, or enough art they can pitch somewhere, to justify the massive expense of prioritizing its creation. They spend their days at their desks, take their meals to-go back to their rooms. When I see them in the halls and ask how it's going, they sigh a lot. The question of value hovers over them, a dark cloud.

On the last night of their program, the writers emerge from their rooms for one last night at the bar. The evening is melancholy and wine-soaked. They leave early the next morning on the same bus.

Later that day, in the dining hall, a flock of jazz musicians lands in their place. They are all younger than me, intimidatingly stylish. They all seem to know each other, speak in a common, melodic language. Their vitality and excitement freak me out. I get my sandwich to go and bring it back to the boat. I sit down at the computer and stare at the screen until my retinas start to scintillate, deleting my lack of a novel, sentence by sentence by sentence.

I still have a month of time alone with my failed ambitions. I try to use it productively. I watch whole seasons of TV and take notes on everything I see, thinking maybe I can eventually turn my thoughts into essays. I take fragmented notes on my emotional state, thinking maybe I can turn them into poetry. I wonder whether I am lying to myself. It is genuinely impossible to tell. I pace around the forest. I walk into town to check out its strange, unsatisfying mall, or visit its one movie theatre alone. I avoid everyone's eyes in the dining hall, go whole days without speaking to another human.

One afternoon I am sitting in the boat, eating a thing of Kraft Dinner I made with the electric kettle and watching a glitching episode of *Drag Race* on the forest's unstable wi-fi, when I hear approaching footsteps from outside. At first I assume it's just the elk or a few stray painters, but as the sound gets closer I can make out what sounds like a group of people, murmuring quietly.

These are the studios, someone is saying. *There are eleven of them, each designed by a different architect, each occupied by a different artist. I think they're all full right now.*

When I look out the window I can see a young man leading a tour group of what look like businesspeople through the forest. Some of them have windbreakers on; a few of them are holding binoculars. They are all squinting in my general direction as their guide explains the rich history of the Artists' Colony. One guy raises his binoculars so he can see inside my porthole. I am wearing a pair of men's underwear and a blanket I brought over from my bedroom around my shoulders like a cape. I duck down below the glass and pull the blanket all the way around me. If the guy can see in, he will hopefully mistake me for a piece of furniture or a pile of garbage, waiting to be swept up and carried away. I stay on the floor until long after the voices have disappeared.

A few hours later an email drops into my inbox. It is from an editor at a large magazine, congratulating me on the publication of my breakout debut novel. He asks if I might be interested in setting up an interview. They must have sent it to the wrong address. I delete the message and press the play button again.

The next day, I get another message from another editor. *Congratulations!* it says. I pause for a split second before hitting delete.

For the next two weeks, I get different versions of this same email. At first they come every few days, then daily, then a few times per afternoon. They are from agents, reporters, bloggers. *Congratulations!* they all say. According to them, my debut work of fiction has finally been sold to a major publisher after a massive bidding war and is already receiving rave reviews in advance of its release. Everyone is astounded at my success, especially because I'm so young.

I know what's going on here. The Emma Healey they are trying to interview is a British author, just a few years older than I am, who shares my name but does not yet have a personal website, so if you search for her you end up finding me. I wonder whether this is the kind of thing the SEO brothers could help her with.

I first became aware of the other Emma Healey a year ago, when a friend who was interning for a large publisher told me she'd sat in on the marketing meeting for my new book, and that she was so excited to hear about my success. I wrote back to her and explained that there must be a mix-up. *Wow, I'm so sorry, that's so weird*, she said, *wow*.

My friends at home say the same thing when I send them screenshots of this new batch of congratulatory emails. *Maybe you should just change your name now and save yourself the trouble,* one of them says, with a casual cruelty that will echo in my mind for the next ten years.

Instead, I start replying to the emails. If they come with interview questions I answer them as thoroughly and honestly as I can before explaining that I am a Canadian poet. It is fun to answer questions about what inspires me, what my habits and routines are. *Oh wow,* everyone says when they get my replies, *So sorry! My mistake!* I post screenshots of these exchanges on social media whenever they come up. It feels almost like doing real work.

One day, after I put up one of these posts, the newspaper editor who edits my book reviews sends me a message. *You have to write about this.*

Yes yes yes yes yes I reply, before I have the chance to think about it. It's just such a relief to have a job.

I am immediately consumed by the task of getting this piece exactly right. Every day for the next week I wake up early and stay up late, furiously writing and rewriting what is supposed to be a 1,500-word feature on my feelings about sharing a name with someone who has my ideal career. I envision it as a hybrid of personal essay and interview—I want to read the other Emma's book and then talk to her about it so I can interpolate my own perspective with hers, bounce back and forth between our life stories, our relationships with form and craft, outlining a subtler thesis about the fractured nature of identity. I have the book delivered to the Centre and contact its author.

The interview goes fine, but the rest of it is difficult. I want to say something about work, identity, value, perception, but I can't quite untangle my thoughts; every time I say something it's not quite what I mean. I try the method I default to when I'm stuck on a poem: free-writing pages and pages of text, trying to wring every single idea out of my mind in the hopes of eventually sifting one good line from the pile. I write about the look in my former professor's eye when I saw him from across the dining hall. I write about men telling me to never use the word "I" in a poem; about taking a class with the lights dimmed so they wouldn't aggravate the professor's hangover; about the stories the real writers used to tell me about defending each other from student complaints at union meetings, in front of disciplinary boards, to each other's girlfriends and wives. I write about realizing you are just one on a never-ending conveyor belt of you. I write and write and write and a whole week moves around me like air.

The finished piece is fragmented, moody and strange. It is achingly personal to me, even though it is only three pages long and half of it is quotes from the other Emma Healey. I have never written anything like it before. When I put it in an email to the Books editor I can hear my heart pounding in my ears. When I click Send I feel like I am standing on the edge of a diving board with my eyes closed, about to jump.

An hour later, he emails me back. *Hey Emma,* the message begins, and my stomach immediately tightens. *Yeah, I think we need another draft. I really, really, really wanted*—and then I stop reading. A light flips on in my brain. I don't need to see anything else to understand the mistake I've made; this is a piece for the *newspaper.* No one opens up the Books section on a Sunday morning to read a poet's scattered, dark, experimental piece about why someone else is more famous than her, and what that has to do with the men who were supposed to teach her how to write.

I stay up all night fixing the essay. In the morning I have something good, charming, easy to read. It sounds like me, or a version of me—the one that talks to new people at parties, or speaks into the microphone at a reading. It has a beginning, a middle and an end. I am proud of it, the kind of pride you'd feel if you built a chair you could actually sit in.

I send the Books editor this new draft, and he loves it. *Exactly what I wanted,* he says. I hide the first one in a folder inside a folder inside a folder that I will never, ever look into again. The paper runs the piece, and then my time at the Centre is over.

My experience in the boat gives me a little momentum. I write book reviews for the newspaper with a new kind of confidence. I pitch a few more essays to places I've never been published before, and some of them get accepted. I write for literary magazines and websites and websites designed to read like literary magazines. I write about a reality show where people pretend to be other people on the internet for dating or revenge, and about a comedy TV show that turns the tropes of reality shows into performance art. I write about songs I like and books I read and what it's like to write fake blog posts for a living. I publish one poem, a version of the one I could never finish in my final year at school, in a small magazine. It's still not right, but a small quarterly takes it anyway. I give the musician one copy and keep the other for myself. His sits on the lower shelf of his bedside table, gathering dust. I pretend not to notice.

The SEO job makes writing hard. At the end of an eight-hour shift extolling the virtues of the best concrete resurfacing Toronto has to offer, all words and ideas are basically the same, just units of language leaning up against each other. I want, very badly, to quit—so when a friend tells me that an art gallery-slash-gift shop near my house is hiring a copywriter, I am flooded with a mixture of desperate panic and relief. This is the job I *need*, the one that will save me.

The gallery shows cool, colourful art by local painters, and sells toys and clothes they bring over from Japan and mark up at a high rate. They are looking for someone to write blog posts and newsletters for their online store. I spend weeks working on my application, designing a website for my portfolio, squinting at my fake posts, going over them again and again like they're poems. I read every product description on the gallery's website, quiz myself on all the most obscure designers they carry. When they call me in for an interview, I spend hours trying to choose an outfit that will convey the right balance of professionalism and whimsy. When they tell me I'm hired, I cry like someone I love has died. I quit the SEO job immediately. The brothers do not take it well. I don't care. I'm free.

The gallery owners are opening up a pop-up shop in an office tower in the heart of the city. They ask me to meet them there late in the evening so we can talk about the job. I have always loved this building; it's an art deco smoked-glass prism that looks antique, like a remnant of a different skyline.

By the time I arrive, the sun is sinking, and the building looks almost liquid in the dusk. Dark amber glass, soft yellow glow from the inside. I can see my reflection in the building, double-exposed against the city. I walk inside, press the button for the elevator and travel up, up, up, into my future.

The gallery is co-owned by a man and a woman. They have been in business together for a very long time and may once have been a couple, even, I can't quite tell. The energy between them is tense and exhausted at the same time. Sometimes I feel like a piece of furniture they've placed strategically between them to dampen the vibe.

Four or five days a week, I come in to work while they move in and out of the building, taking phone calls. I sit in a folding chair at a white desk in a completely empty room at the back of the gallery. The sound of my typing clatters off the white walls, shattering the quiet. I write the newsletter, update the website, make blog posts that might get people to click through. My big innovation is writing "product horoscopes" for the newsletter, which are exactly what they sound like:

Aries, it's no secret that you're the life of the party. When friends need a little extra excitement in their lives, you're the one they turn to. But sometimes even the biggest party animals need a little break—nothing major, just a little downtime to reflect and recharge. Give your-self some breathing space this month; you'll need your energy for all the amazing parties waiting for you in December. This [stuffed animal for adults] will keep you company at home, the new issue of [$20 art magazine] will give you something to read while you kick back and relax, and these [Garfield-themed ankle socks] are just plain awesome.

One afternoon, I'm in the middle of describing a piece of Lucite jewellery when one of the owners comes into the back room, shuffling a thick stack of mail like a deck of tarot cards. After a long pause she tears one letter open, lets the envelope drop to the floor, and squints at the notice inside. Then she looks up at me like she's just realized I'm in the room. *You know*, she says, *people think running a place like this is easy. But it's not. It's not easy at all.* I'm not sure what to say, so I nod. Three weeks later, she tells me they can no longer afford to pay me.

Some people online are talking about a news story. A man in America, a peripheral figure in an insular literary community, has been leveraging his status within the community to manipulate, harass and assault younger women. One woman has posted a story about her experience with him, and now others are beginning to tell theirs. Stitched together, the accounts are eerily consistent—like the women are all describing a collective dream whose details shift, but whose core plot points are always the same. That's the part I can't stop thinking about. The symmetry.

I ask a friend who edits a blog if I can write about it. My first draft is a thoughtful and extremely long piece about systems and patriarchy and perception—about how a man with a tiny amount of power can end up exerting such a tremendous amount of influence over the lives of so many people, and how so many communities are quietly designed to tacitly uphold and perpetuate this kind of manipulation.

The piece is fine. Reading it is like chewing a perfectly edible but entirely dry cracker. I send it, and a day later my editor replies. She says it really seems like there is a reason this story is bothering me so much, and right now she can't tell what that reason is. She adds that she doesn't want me to write about anything I'm not comfortable with. But I already know what I want to say.

I write just what I remember. I keep the story small-scale: one relationship, one person, one night. I try to make it clear, concise, coherent, moving straight from a beginning to an end. When I'm done, I read it over. My editor was right. The details make it real.

A few days later I'm at the movies alone, watching the previews, when an email blinks up on my phone: the piece has been cleared by their lawyers. The word *lawyers* sends a strobe of panic through me. I let it dissolve.

They publish it the next day. I watch it go up on the website, reread it for typos a few times before posting the link on social media. For an hour nothing happens. I get up, make some tea, wander around the apartment straightening the pictures on my walls. I'm not sure what I expect to happen. Time passes. Then my phone starts to vibrate.

It sounds the way the rain sounds against your window at the start of a thunderstorm: a few small sounds, then a few more. Then a crescendo. The messages are in my inbox, on my phone, in my voicemail, my DMs. They are from strangers and friends and acquaintances, old teachers and co-workers, my parents' friends. My phone's battery dies before I can even read them all. I plug it in and sit on the floor, staring down at the screen.

The messages vary in form, tone and content. Some are apologetic. Some are furious. A few are perversely gleeful. Men who went to my university, or taught there, or worked with the real writers, helpfully let me know they always knew those guys were creeps. Strangers who have never met me write to tell me I'm a liar.

But most of them are just stories that sound almost exactly like the one I wrote. Some overflow with detail. Some are sparse as erasure. At first I try to write back to everyone. I say *thank you, I'm sorry, thank you, I'm sorry. I'm sorry. I'm sorry.* It's not enough, and soon I fall so far behind I'll never catch up again.

The parts that make me cry are never the most graphic or horrifying details. It's the tiny things. The colour of the paint on the walls. The clothes they were wearing. The words. I spend the day reading these messages, bent over my phone until I can't feel my body anymore.

I get a new job off Kijiji as a receptionist at a massage therapy clinic. The place is run by a mother and daughter who hate each other. The mother is always dropping in without notice, rearranging the decor, fucking up the day's receipts, distracting the customers. The daughter is always trailing behind her, cleaning up the mess. I feel bad for them both but also secretly enjoy their dynamic; it's like being an insignificant character in someone else's TV show.

I like everything about this job. I like the other receptionist, who is an aspiring self-help author so strikingly beautiful that clients do actual double takes when they see her behind the desk. I like the individually wrapped squares of chocolate we keep in a little bowl on the desk in front of me. I like the rhythm of pulling patient files and the puzzle of filing an insurance claim. I like folding sheets in the laundry room, which always smells like lavender and fresh air. I like the clinic's decor, whose central theme is INSPIRATIONAL WORDS—like the wall hanging that says DREAM in big loopy cursive letters above the front doorway. I like calling each therapist to tell them their schedule for the next day at the end of this one. Crossing everything off the list, reducing the day down and down and down.

The best time at the clinic is closing, when everybody leaves and I can plug my iPod into the stereo. I have a few little routines. My favourite one comes after I've closed out all the insurance claims, set up all the charts, folded all the towels, cashed out the till, made all the phone calls and poured the dregs of the cucumber-mint water into the kitchen sink. When all these tasks are done, I walk into the room with the infrared sauna and just stare at it for a while, wondering if this is the day I'll finally try it out.

The sauna looks like a tiny log cabin with a complex panel of dials and switches on the side, like a time travel device from an '80s movie. On my first day at the clinic, the other receptionist told me it was special because it heats people up from the inside, so they don't have to experience any physical discomfort. *You barely even notice what's happening*, she said.

Like the way they boil frogs? I asked.

Yeah, she said, after thinking about it for a second. *I guess so!*

Part of the reason I am so obsessed with the sauna is that sometimes a guy prank calls the clinic about it. I have a theory that he works for a rival massage therapist, but all my evidence is circumstantial. He always calls saying he wants to book an appointment, and then when I tell him how much it costs, he screams into the phone about our pricing until I hang up. *It's too fucking expensive!* he yells so loud the line glitches. *Don't you know that?*

All of this only adds to the sauna's mysterious appeal. Sometimes, standing in front of it in the weak evening light, I take off a few layers of clothing and dare myself to do more. But something always drags me back into the moment—a pause in the music, or the click and thump of someone locking up the hearing aid clinic downstairs.

The very last thing I do before I leave for the night is check my reflection. In the hallway that leads from the reception area to the treatment rooms, there's a very weird poster pretending to be a mirror. It's made of a reflective paper in which you can *kind of* see your own outline, but just barely. Printed on it is a cascade of words, all different sizes, horizontal and vertical, arranged in little clusters. Every word is a synonym for "health," but the closer you get to the edges of the image, the more abstract the connection becomes. A spectrum of meaning, degrading: *good happy wellbeing contentment robust salubrious hale sanitary vim pow vigour euphoria condition welfare.* There are real mirrors in the clinic, too, but for some reason I like to see myself in this one.

Sexual assault is becoming a hot news item out in the world. There is a market for strong opinions about it. When a local celebrity is publicly accused of committing numerous horrific crimes against women he has dated and worked with, the producers of a morning show on the national broadcaster's radio station invite me and another young essayist to come on at six in the morning and talk about it.

I take a cab downtown to the office tower where they make the news. The building is labyrinthine inside, disorienting. It's so early that the building is almost empty of people. I walk through three eerily empty newsrooms before I find the room I'm looking for. The other essayist is already there. Her hair is shiny and her makeup is perfect even though it's still dark outside; she works an office job at a publishing company, she explains, so she's used to getting up early.

The show is broadcast out of a small, white-walled studio, with one enormous window built in on one side so the producers can see what the host is doing. I have heard this man's voice coming through the radio in my own home a million different times. In person he's smaller and more fine-featured than I ever imagined—he looks a bit like the tiny wax groom on a wedding cake. It is strange to see an intimately familiar voice coming out of a total stranger's mouth.

The essayist and I sit next to each other. The host makes clear and direct eye contact with each of us, one at a time. He asks what we think should be done about abuses of power in small professional communities. When I answer, I can't help but picture my voice being broadcast out over the city—to people in their cars, people in their kitchens. I barely notice what I'm saying, and then the interview's over.

A week later, I get an email from two editors who work with the young essayist at the large publishing house. They tuned in to the radio show to listen to her and heard me. They want to know if I can come in to talk.

The large publisher's headquarters are located in a large office tower downtown. The walls are bright white. In the meeting room, there is a framed screen-print by a local artist, a reproduction of one of the publisher's iconic book covers. The editors want to know whether I might be interested in pitching a book about imbalances of power, systemic abuse. They envision it as a building out of the ideas in my essay, a kind of contemporary feminist manifesto. They were particularly interested, they say, in a thing I mentioned on the radio about *finally being able to believe myself.* They think it might be a good jumping-off point. I tell them I am definitely interested, and the rest of the meeting is a blur. I go home with a knot of fear pulling tight in my gut.

Here's the problem: I can't remember saying anything on the radio about believing myself. I don't know if that statement is even true. Ever since I published that essay my memories feel unreliable, filmy, difficult to grasp. The pressure of making them public has done something to my mind. I don't want to trick the editors or disappoint them, but also, this is the biggest professional opportunity I have ever been offered. Is it worse to let them think I possess a kind of insight that I don't, or to tell them up front that I'm not the person they think I am and blow my shot?

For days, I draft the email in my head. Pacing the apartment, walking the block, making dinner, lying in bed. Sometimes I even get close to sending it—on the couch with my laptop on my knees and my hands hovering over the keyboard, I imagine typing *I'm sorry. I don't know if I'm the person you're looking for.* Then I imagine deleting it. Eventually I realize that I can look up the archive of the show online and play it back. I can feel my heart fluttering as I press the play button. A few minutes in, I hear a woman's voice:

I think it's gotten easier for me to believe myself, believe in the truth of my own experience.

I don't remember those words coming out of my mouth, but there they are. Someone is saying them and she is me. I pull back the play bar and listen again, repeat the gesture until the words disintegrate into syllables, until the syllables break into sound.

I spend months trying to write the pitch. The editors tell me that if I can sell it, the advance will be enough for me to live off for maybe six months. It would be more money than I've ever made before.

I write thousands of words, tens of thousands, drafts on drafts on drafts. In each one, I sound like someone is strangling an opinion out of me. The limits of my perspective feel tight around my mind.

The editors try to help me. They are patient. We talk on the phone. I send more drafts and they send notes. I do not want to fail at this. I want to leave my cramped apartment and my silent boyfriend and my imaginary novel and vault myself into another life. All I need to do this is to take all the experiences I have had as a woman and form a coherent, overarching thesis about them that will make people want to know more. I am frustrated with my brain's inability to process my life experiences into valuable material. Who knows when I will get an opportunity like this again?

Part of the problem is maybe that whenever I sit down to write, I end up daydreaming. Mostly I try to imagine what the book would look like. A thin softcover with my name on it, something that fits easily into a small bag. A nice author photo of me looking serious. I imagine searching my own name for reviews and reading them one by one while hot acid boils in my stomach. I imagine my phone in the palm of my hand, buzzing until the battery dies. I think of the moments in my life when I have had the least control over my body: in his bed or mine, in the bar, closing, on the street outside, lying on my back in the grass, not able to move. I remember how each time it happened, I felt joined to the versions of me that had lived it before.

Like maybe this was the full purpose of my life, and nothing else that happened to me would ever actually matter.

I tell the editors I can't write the pitch. They are nice about it, say to keep in touch.

When the musician and I break up, neither of us wants to keep the apartment.

A few weeks later, I get a call from the other receptionist at work. The mother accidentally flooded the whole building by leaving the washing machine on overnight with the door open. No one knows when the clinic will open again. Just like that, I'm a writer and nothing else.

FOUR

One week, instead of going to the Cineplex, we see a movie Deragh made with another friend of hers.

The film is about distance and memory. The plot focuses on an archive of letters the filmmaker's grandmother once wrote to a famous poet, which are currently held in the library of a prestigious American university. The film's protagonist, played by Deragh, travels to the university to read them, and spends her time there thinking about and discussing their contents with various people.

The film's relationship with reality is complex. The archive, the letters and the grandmother are all real, but Deragh is playing a fictional character who is like the filmmaker, but also not like her at all.

The letters are written in a language she doesn't understand, and not all of them have been translated. For much of the film Deragh sits at a long wooden table, reading and taking sparse notes we cannot see. Sometimes we just watch her handling paper for long, silent stretches of time. It is mesmerizing to watch someone so absorbed in their work.

In one scene, she brings some of the letters into a special darkened room with an overhead projector and places them onto the glass. It is a beautiful image. The envelopes glow, the postmarks glow, the paper glows. Her hands seem almost transparent as she touches the letters, moves them across the screen. All that evidence, turning realer and more dreamlike in the light.

I move into an apartment in the neighbourhood where I grew up. When I was a child, the area was called Little Poland, and the main street was lined with barbers and butchers and bars. Now those storefronts house expensive florists and boutique olive oil shops. The pharmacy around the corner from my mom's house is being converted into an exercise studio for children, and the old Goodwill is now a salvage shop that resells antique glass bottles and harvest tables from estate sales at ten times their original price.

A few relics from the neighbourhood's old life remain, maybe because they are too cumbersome to remove—like the huge bronze statue of Pope John Paul II across from the library, always decorated with flowers and candles at the base. Neighbourhood children climb on his outstretched arms in the summertime, eat ten-dollar cones of ice cream at his feet.

My new house is enormous, airy, and collapsing from the outside in. It has a gigantic backyard and a rotting patio and peeling paint and bright sunlight coming through the thin windows of every room. Much of the decor is from the '70s: the kitchen tiling has a beige-yellow-brown hedgehog motif and there are cutting boards built into the counters. The bathroom is all rich, ancient wood panelling, like an antique sauna. The hardwood floors creak under my feet.

My bedroom is really more the idea of a room than an actual private space; the wall that separates it from the hallway is really just a long, accordion-hinged closet door. I position my mattress under the window, a single pane of ancient glass with a hole so big I can fit both my thumbs through it. At the other end of the room, an antique washer and dryer sit behind a curtain. I watch it ripple in the breeze.

I have two roommates, friends of friends, one of them also named Emma—a willowy, pale academic with elegant tattoos that climb like ivy up her arms. This Emma is doing a PhD in dance criticism and has been in the house the longest, so she gets the bedroom upstairs with the en suite. She and her ex-husband share custody of their dog, a hyperactive, blue-eyed Australian Shepherd named Levi who loses his shit at absolutely everything. On the weeks he lives with us, his high-pitched bark rattles my eardrums—but when he's gone, the house feels far too quiet.

My other roommate, Layne, has dark hair in a blunt bob and a laugh like a room full of bright lights flicking on. The day after I move in, she drives me to IKEA so I can buy new furniture for my room and then spends all night helping me build it.

Layne works part-time at a fancy hotel a few days a week, but the rest of the time she is a curator. She organizes site-specific art shows around the city, mostly in abandoned or underused buildings: salt domes and power-generating stations, the kinds of places you pass by and think *I wonder what's in there*. As I get to know her, I will learn that Layne's version of this city has a dimension mine lacks. She knows more about its history than anyone else I've met: the river that runs under the sidewalk in our neighbourhood, the landfill dumped in the lake to make the theme park on the shore. Her mind is an encyclopedia of what everything used to be, what it is, what it will someday become.

Right now, she tells me, property is at a premium. All over the city, loft buildings, artists' studios and industrial buildings are getting bought up by developers who evict the current tenants so they can gut, raze and rebirth the spaces as expensive condos.

Sometimes, a few weeks before one of these buildings is torn down, a small art exhibit will flare to life inside. The work in these shows often uses the space to address the city's rapid gentrification, but their commentary is complicated by the fact that the spaces are also financed by the developers themselves; a little gesture of pity cloaked in a demonstration of power, or maybe the other way around. The art show is a ceremony that marks a building's passage from one world into the next. It is never permanent, always a pop-up. The building always has to be made useful eventually.

Layne tells me all of this as we assemble my bedframe; I watch her hair fall forward around her face as she Allen-keys together planks of medium-density fibreboard. She's good at building things. I think, for the first of what will be hundreds of thousands of times in my life, that I'm lucky to know her.

When the bed's finished, I lie down to test it, and notice a sliver of light from the hallway leaking in from under my closet-door wall. The next morning, when I wake up, I realize the wall is basically cosmetic. Everything in the house sounds like it is happening inside my room: the dog's frantic bark, Emma grinding coffee in the kitchen, cars rushing down the street outside. Above me, I can feel cool air coming in through the glass.

A friend's husband tells me his office is looking for a copywriter. He heard I'm looking for work, and they need someone to start in January. When he asks if I might be interested I say *Yes please* immediately, even though I don't really know what his company does. I look it up later, at home; it's a speaker's agency. I don't really know what that is, but the interview goes well, and suddenly I am employed.

On New Year's Eve, I go to a friend's DJ night. It is an excellent party: I'm dancing, laughing, wearing a good dress, lit up with the promise of future income. Just after midnight, a man I vaguely recognize sidles up to me; a friend of a friend of a friend who works in my new office. *I hear we're going to be co-workers*, he yells over the Whitney Houston blaring from the speakers. *I guess so!* I say.

A few hours later, when I leave the bar, he runs out after me. *Hey*, he says, his breath rising away from him in the cold. His apartment is fifteen minutes away but it takes us half an hour to walk there, picking our way through the slush and ice.

On my first day at the new office, my friend's husband—now my manager—walks me to my desk. When I get there, I discover that I'll be sitting next to the man from New Year's Eve. He is, in fact, the agency's only other copywriter. We will be working together on everything. I didn't know this, but from the sheepish way he grins up at me as we're being introduced, I can tell he did.

The agency represents authors and "thinkers" and "analysts" and "futurists" and "consultants" and comedians and filmmakers and designers and life coaches, plus a wide range of B- and C- and D-list public figures. For fees that range from a few hundred to hundreds of thousands of dollars, they will send a professional lecturer to your conference to deliver a speech.

Almost all of the talks are centred around the same handful of terms: *leadership, communication, inspiration, disruption*. They begin with a personal anecdote, or a hypothetical question, or an interesting fact, before shifting to a thesis that has to do with the nature of the world. These speeches feel personal, but they don't often actually tell you much about the people giving them. The details are polished to a high shine, revealing exactly as much as they need to. Sometimes, while I am listening to a lecture, I try to picture its speaker at home, sitting at their desk, figuring out what parts of their life might fit best inside the form, stripping the rest away.

The speeches are practically identical in their structure. Once you've heard one of them, you can listen to any other and know precisely when the pauses will occur, when the jokes will be strategically inserted, when the speaker will turn from telling you a story to telling you about what that story means. The repetitiveness is comforting. Whether a speaker is talking about a scientific discovery, a personal tragedy, or the line of their whole life, it always takes the same shape. By my second week at the agency I am certain I'll be able to access this rhythm long after my mind has ceased to retain all other useful information or personal memories, the same way I can still sing advertising jingles from my childhood.

The "creatives" sit together on the outskirts of the office, while the agents sit in a tight nest at the centre of the space. The agents seem much older than us, though they are mostly about the same age—they dress true Business Casual and are always about to get married or buy a house. All day you can hear them making phone calls, bird-calling their clients in charm language, *just following up!* The owner of the company sits in his own corner, sectioned off from everyone else by soft dividers that do little to muffle the sounds of his phone meetings, or his habit of clipping his nails at his desk.

I sit between the New Year's Eve guy and a woman named Trish, who manages the agency's website. Trish has a luminous smile and an easy laugh and she brings fresh fruit every day to slice, arrange on a plate, and share with the rest of us around 4:00 p.m. because *that's the time of day when your blood sugar gets low*, she explains. Everyone is a little in love with her, but especially me.

As a copywriter, I write—and alter—speakers' biographies. Clients come to the agency with an empty space in a conference that needs filling, and the agents suggest a shortlist of potential speakers that might fit their needs. I take those shortlists and put together a package of information on all the speakers that the agent can then send back to the client, in order to help them decide.

A large part of the job is being able to describe the same thing five or six different ways: for example, if a speaker has only one talk about how they overcame a horrific childhood trauma in order to become a millionaire neurosurgeon, I can frame it as an inspirational talk about perseverance in the face of unspeakable adversity, or an educational talk about the mechanics of rising through the ranks of a difficult industry, or a lightly scientific examination of the human mind. A lot depends, I am learning, on the angle from which you choose to tell a story.

There's this database that everyone in the office has access to, with listings for each speaker the agency has ever represented. When I click on any name, I can see the minimum amount of money they charge per speech, plus any relevant notes about their requirements. The more in-demand or expert a speaker is, the more luxuries and accommodations they can comfortably request. Some people fly only first class, or they need a specific per diem along with their speaking fee; these people generally work less, because fewer clients can afford them. Speakers who work cheaper do less glamorous gigs, but more often. There is also a class of speaker whose insights are considered so valuable that almost no one can afford to hear them; these are mostly actual celebrities, who often have better things to do. A few names in the database come with a note that says the agency has tried to convince them to try public speaking, but they simply will not give talks, no matter how much money they are offered. Some people's opinions can't be bought. But not many.

I use the database about ten million times per day. At the end of every proposal and pitch, I paste in the speaker's fees and requirements so that clients can have a better idea of what it's going to cost them. Some days, to kill time, I'll flip through the archive, looking up random B- and C-list celebrities to see how much everyone's words are worth. The results are often surprising. One famous movie star is happy to fly coach, while a writer with only one real published book demands an extra $10,000 to travel on weekends and requires a private car for the duration of his trip. It is nearly impossible to understand the equations people use to calculate their own value.

My salary at the agency is not much more than I made with the SEO brothers, but it doesn't take long for me to start spending it like I'm never going to have to look for work again. I buy breakfast when I'm running late in the morning and order takeout when I come home tired. I buy a subway pass at the beginning of every month. I buy produce from the place around the corner that marks it up a little bit, instead of the busy grocery store five blocks away. I buy drinks at the bar and cabs to get me back home and Tylenol and weed for the next day's hangover. I buy two separate decks of tarot cards and an appliance that turns plain tap water into sparkling. I buy two bras that fit, I get my winter boots resoled, I think seriously about getting a cat, and I go to the thrift store every weekend. When I walk through the sliding doors I feel like those ancient Greek priestesses who used to take drugs and then flash out of time into a mystical vision, looking forward and backward all at once. I transmit myself into a purely evaluative state, merging with the shelves crammed with housewares and the racks full of clothing. Material, texture, colour. My life gets thicker. Lush.

A woman stands on a stage. It looks like the set of a low-budget children's TV show. Behind her there are shelves filled with all the items a fictional smart kid's bedroom would contain: piles of books, a microscope, a globe. The video is not great quality; you can see the EXIT signs glowing at the edges of the stage. The backs of many balding, white heads float before her in the audience. She is wearing slacks and a pink polo shirt with the logo of her organization embroidered on the breast. There is a screen next to her. Her voice is strong but it cracks in emotional moments.

As she speaks, a man walks out onto the stage with a tray. On the tray is a real human brain, severed neatly into two hemispheres. A spinal cord dangles from the end; its bounciness evokes a loose phone cord. As she speaks, the woman picks up both halves of the brain, one in each hand, and begins to rotate it, pointing at different areas. "This half processes the past and the future," she explains, "while the other is all about the present moment."

She is telling us this so we can understand the story of the blood clot that exploded inside her own head. She describes the experience of looking down at her body and no longer recognizing it, as the part of her mind that understood the past and future shut down completely. In that moment, she says, she felt as though she had merged with the world around her—like there was no difference between her and anything else. Just a continuous present.

For a while it's fun. The other copywriter and I slide notes to each other across our desks, kiss in the empty elevator after the doors close. When I get up in the morning to dress for work, I pick my outfits as though I am playing the role of a person who works in an office and is secretly sleeping with her co-worker. I like seeing myself this way, playing this role.

He does too. When he looks at me, I see him looking at the idea of a woman he should be dating, who he deserves or is destined to be with. I can feel her moving across me like a projection on a screen. In the office I watch his face as he texts her. When I respond, I think about what she might say. When we go to the record store together after work, I catch him watching her flip through the New Arrivals. When I speak, I can watch him hearing the story of her, thinking about how she fits into his life. When we fuck, she's so close I can reach out and touch her.

Some nights after work, Trish and I go to the only cheap bar in the neighbourhood. Over the stereo, we yell at each other about our other jobs, partners past and present, office gossip. The gimmick of this bar is that the whole place is just half the width of a regular building; you have to turn yourself sideways, Flat Stanley–style, to walk through. Bartenders blast the kinds of pop-punk songs I loved in high school over the stereo, the tables are dented and carved and covered in layers of peeling paint, and every surface is sticky with Corona. The air smells like lime juice and bleach. I like the bar, but I like leaving it more. When I step out onto the sidewalk I always feel newly sensitive to the size of the world—its width and range, its openness. It's like I'm experiencing it for the first time.

Other evenings, I meet up with a friend of a friend who works in an office down the street from the agency. We discovered this coincidence at a party, not long after I started working there. *We should hang out after work*, she said. *Do you do hot yoga?* I said yes not because I ever had, but because it seemed like something someone with a full-time salaried job would enjoy.

The studio is just around the corner, on the second floor of an ugly concrete building, up a narrow flight of stairs. The light inside is soft, the air smells like sandalwood, the walls are white, the classes are expensive, and the locker rooms are tiny. Watching a cramped room full of women struggling into and out of their workout clothes, checking their phones while naked, bumping into each other while trying not to make eye contact and secretly staring while blow-drying their hair is the only genuinely relaxing part of the class.

The room where they heat you up is enormous, with mirrors along the walls and beautiful pale wood floorboards so glossy you can see your reflection in them. My friend is very, very good at hot yoga. I catch people around us watching her with admiration and envy during the difficult poses. I sweat conspicuously all over my rented mat, gasp for breath during the hard poses, and make a lot of noise when I fall down. Everyone says *Namaste* at the end, which makes me uncomfortable, because everyone in the room including the teacher is white. I mouth along silently, a stupid compromise. The whole thing is humiliating.

But after, on the sidewalk in the cold evening air, sweat drying in trails along my body, I have to admit that I feel weightless. Like every feeling has been wrung out of my body by an expensive, efficient machine. I go home and sleep better than I ever have before in my life.

My new bedroom is big enough to fit a desk, which feels like a thrilling novelty, even if it is just a big piece of particle board suspended on two legs I pulled from the neighbours' trash. The office job doesn't afford me a lot of time to pitch or write long essays, but I still have time to do a little freelancing on the weekends. There is a burgeoning market for clear, straightforward, inoffensively feminist interpretations of the news; famous men are being accused of assaulting their employees or their students or their peers with increasing frequency, and sometimes editors will ask me if I want to write an opinion piece about it. My opinion is always that it's bad.

Eventually, an editor at a city paper offers me the chance to write for them on a semi-regular basis, covering a wider range of topics from a more generally feminist angle. The pieces take between a day and three to write, depending on my ability to focus; I do one every couple of weeks. I spend these weekends hunched over my laptop, researching the stories that make the front pages of the paper and trying to determine which of my opinions about them are interesting. *How should this music festival handle protests over a performer's misogynist lyrics? What should we take from the famous man's acquittal? How are we feeling about abortions these days?* Once these pieces are published I never read them again, but I do post links to them on my personal website in case anyone else ever wants to, which seems unlikely. I like watching the titles accumulate. I have a vague sense that when I pass a certain number something will happen, though I'm not sure what.

The voice I use in these pieces is concise and clear, like the opening remarks by a talented high school debate team captain. The structure is always the same: introduction, swift tour through the relevant details, a clear opinion, stick the landing. I try to make my strongest points in a rhythm that might get caught in a reader's mind. If you look at one of these pieces by itself, you might think I'm a competent writer—but if you looked at them all in a row, you would think maybe you were engaging with a conceptual art project or the work of a very well-programmed robot, outlining the same ideas in slightly different terms, filling the space that needs filling.

I make $250, after taxes, for each piece. Two hundred and fifty dollars is exactly what it is and nothing else. It is both a lot of money and almost nothing. You can spend it in your sleep and you'd be stupid to turn it down, especially if all you need to do in order to acquire it is express an opinion you already have. But it is also foolish to spend more than twelve cumulative hours working on something for a paycheque that will disappear out of your bank account before you've even had the chance to notice it was there. The more time I spend on each idea, the less each one is worth.

Every "creative" at the speaker's agency is responsible for covering the front desk once a week so the receptionist can take her break. I am just as abysmal with the phone at this job as I was when I worked as an intern—I stumble over basic phrases, haven't memorized our address, patch calls through to the wrong lines, overcomplicate even the most basic conversations.

People call the front desk for two reasons: because they forgot the extension of the employee they're supposed to talk to, or because they want to pitch themselves as speakers. Most of the callers in the latter category are self-styled gurus or self-published authors or aspiring influencers who've heard from somewhere that public speaking pays a lot of money. They are not wrong, but the job at reception is to politely inform them that we don't take pitches over the phone and direct them to an email address I don't think anyone actually checks.

It is hard to perform this redirection. The callers have learned from watching the kinds of speeches we sell that being relentless in the pursuit of one's dreams is the best way to realize them; no matter how many times I tell them I have no power to help, they persist. When I hang up the phone after these conversations I always feel a little grimy, like the guilt is a physical thing settling over my skin.

A woman stands onstage in a pool of silver light. She is talking about her quest to create building materials that regenerate like organic material. Behind her, a computer-generated image of a chair built of silvery spiderweb stuff blooms into itself. "Eventually," she says, "we will have a city that responds to natural conditions the way that plants do; that rebuilds itself like a body, healing."

One night, the other copywriter and I go to the movies. It is the kind of deep winter night where everything in the city is layered in frozen slush. It's like standing on the surface of the moon. We smoke a joint huddled together in an alley behind the theatre. The office buildings sway almost imperceptibly in the high wind, their windows glowing warm orange.

We see one of those movies about a man trying to solve a mystery. He travels from scene to scene tracing its edges but can't ever solve it, maybe because there's no solution.

In one scene, he's in love with a beautiful woman, walking through the city in the pouring rain. They are looking for something together and can't find it, but it doesn't really matter. They stop their search next to a construction site—a fenced-off lot of empty land, not yet developed, just a strange gap in the city. Their hair is soaked, their clothes are soaked, and she is barefoot for some reason. They duck into a doorframe and kiss in the warm glow of a neon sign. It is a beautiful scene, a perfect memory. Months or years later, when the protagonist returns to that same site, there is a sleek glass office tower standing where that open space used to be.

Later that night, lying in his bed, the other copywriter and I are comparing first impressions of each other. He mentions, in a tone that's supposed to sound casual, that before I started working at the office our manager sent around some links to essays I'd written, as a kind of introduction. After that, he says, he looked up some more of my writing. A wave of panic passes reflexively through me, turning my body to static.

Oh yeah? I ask. *What did you think of it?*

I thought it was alright, he says, not looking at me. *Not bad, but not really my thing.*

A speaker is describing a device she puts on her tongue every day. It is attached to a sensor on her forehead that turns light into small electrical impulses. After weeks of use, it has been able to retrain her brain to recognize visual input through a pathway that is not her optic nerves. She describes the experience of walking down a crowded street, where she can now recognize the shapes of buildings, the colours of nearby cars. Your body can adapt to almost anything, she explains. There is more than one way to see.

I download an app that turns dating into a game. Each time you sign in you're shown a stack of profiles, piled on top of each other like a deck of cards, and then you swipe through them one by one: *Yes, no, no, no, yes.* This structure creates the illusion of moving in a straight line, always forward, like you're checking items off a to-do list. Played long enough, the game becomes almost meditative. The chats and meetings are entirely beside the point. The core of everything is in the gesture, the repetition, the split-second decision you make now, now, now, now, now. If you do it long enough you can even get all the way to the end of the pile, your own icon flashing its lonely beacon out into the empty world.

The app is immensely popular. I see people swiping through it on the street, in restaurants, in line for coffee. I use it to fill every single free second of my waking life—on the streetcar, in my bed, in the bathroom, on my lunch break. I feel both liberated and hemmed in by the nature of the game, the rhythm of picking people up and discarding them. I spend so many nights exchanging aimless small talk with strange men, trying to discern through their photos and punctuation whether they might murder me. When I get a message my phone flickers in my pocket, two vibrations, *short short.* After a few months of playing the game I start feeling them in my body even when my phone is off, or in the other room. When the subway passes outside my window, or the streetcar shakes the ground beneath my feet, or a muscle in my leg jumps, I think someone must want me.

I take to the form of the first-date conversation like water taking the shape of its container. I like how you can use the most basic facts of your life to sound out the details of someone else's. It's like learning a new kind of grammar. I like trying to figure out the best way to time-release a few key details about myself, watching the other person figure out how to respond. I like each of us chipping away at the structure, trying to see if there's anything we like underneath. After a little practice I can feel these conversations driving themselves, as if I am nothing but a channel for a pattern of call-and-response.

The first question is always *So what do you do?* Every job is exactly the same. People work at the bank, the bookstore, the record store. They do PhDs and graphic design and social media for a brand. They work at bars and restaurants and coffee shops, they're going on tour, they're looking to get out of the industry so they're learning to code. The speaker's agency is not a particularly sexy place, so I develop a habit of talking about my job at the porn company. The story has everything; it can be funny or serious, a little melancholy. When I mention the names of the websites the company owned, I look at my date's face for a reaction, and it gives me a pretty good sense of whether they want to take me home.

Sometimes, when I am having sex with someone I met through the app, I will hear phrases come out of their mouth that I recognize immediately from porn. It makes me feel safe to know we're both pretending a little bit, playing characters. Sex with someone you've known for only a few dates, or a few hours, can be an expansive and terrifying mystery. You can read things that have been written on them for decades, glimpse habits and gestures formed through routes you can barely imagine. But when everyone uses the script, the experience acquires a familiar, safe structure. You can move from beginning to end, safe in knowing you both know your role.

One night, I'm sitting across the table from a perfectly nice young man. *I actually looked up your name after I found you online*, he says.

Oh yeah? I ask.

Yeah. I read a couple of your essays.

Oh yeah?

They were good.

There is a long pause. I know I am supposed to say something to fill it but I can't figure out what. Then he cocks an eyebrow. Goes: *Maybe you can write about me someday.*

"As I'm speaking," the speaker says, "my sound is getting captured by a tablet, and then it's getting mapped onto a vest that's covered in vibratory motors, just like the motors in your cell phone. I'm feeling the sonic world around me."

The screen behind him cuts to a video of two men. One of them is slowly speaking single words to the other, who is writing each of those words on a whiteboard. The man writing, the speaker explains, is profoundly deaf, but the vest is taking the sound of his words and pressing them into his body.

"Jonathan is able to translate this complicated pattern of vibrations into an understanding of what's being said," the speaker says. "After wearing this for about three months, he will have a direct perceptual experience of hearing—in the same way that when a blind person passes a finger over Braille the meaning comes directly off the page, without any conscious intervention at all. They are building a new sense directly into his brain. All it really takes is practice."

I meet a young writer at a party. I already know his name and reputation; his first book came out the same year as mine and was far more successful. Within a few minutes of talking, we figure out that he works in the office across the street from the speaker's agency, that he started his job there on the same day I started mine. I like the symmetry.

The first time we go out for drinks, he confesses he has read my writing. His ex-girlfriend went through the same creative writing program as me, a few years earlier. She knew the poets and professors I knew, had the same late nights out at the bar. She showed him my essay about the program when it came out. They read it together, discussed my experiences, lined them up against hers. Knowing this makes me feel immediately connected to him, even though he is telling me about another person.

I haven't read his book, but I know the gist. The young writer had a difficult childhood and a worse adolescence. When he was a teenager he joined the family business, which involved moving out to a very remote part of the country with his father every summer and working a very difficult industrial job. For two years, the writer spent seasons hauling heavy stuff around with a bunch of other men, then coming home to a motel room where he spent sleepless, sweaty nights reading poetry, masturbating into the thin hotel sheets and punching the walls in fits of teen angst. He saw women only rarely, and each and every one of them ended up in his book. They appear at the edges of his stories—handing the men things in stores, driving tractors across the horizon, flickering in the cheap neon light of bars in town.

When the young writer came back to the world, he went to school for creative writing and published his first book, a series of short stories about work. It was well-reviewed, shortlisted for awards, praised for its thoughtful and nuanced depictions of masculinity. Now he has an office job and writes on weekends. He doesn't mind. *It gives my life structure,* he says. The company he works for has one of those corporate names that sounds exceptionally fake—just two Business Words leaning up against each other, exchanging Business Energy, like GloboTech or PowerCorp. He will explain his job to me at least fifteen more times, but the details will slide off the surface of my brain like eggs off a non-stick pan. I know it has something to do with computers and privacy. It doesn't matter.

We laugh a lot. He is smart, funny and impressed by me. I do not feel wary or nervous or bored; I relax into the conversation, forgetting myself. At the end of the night he pays for my drinks, walks with me for a while, then hails a cab to send me home alone.

After a few weeks, I get to see his apartment. The young writer lives in an enormous loft with high ceilings and shelves full of books. He's subletting the place from a friend of a friend, but even after I learn this, I can't help reading each piece of decor for clues about his personality. The glasses in the cupboards, the fabric on the couch, the sunlight coming through the enormous windows, the view of the city outside. A few things in the apartment are definitely his, like the huge gaming PC with its glowing rainbow keyboard, completely incongruous with the rest of the decor. Others could go either way, like the enormous punching bag that hangs from the ceiling, which he spars with when he's bored.

We develop a routine. After work, I bring my laptop over and sit for hours at the dining room table, typing and deleting different versions of the same sentence, while he does the same thing on the other side of the loft.

He's working on a new book of short stories and I think maybe I'm writing poems again. We email each other new pages, or read paragraphs to each other out loud if we're feeling particularly proud of something we've come up with. I am not used to sharing my writing with another person so early in the process, but I trust him. It feels good. We are each deeply compelled by the idea that we have rare access to the other person's mind; he tells me I'm his best friend, that I understand him better than anyone else in his life, and I believe it. Sometimes I recognize flashes of myself in his stories—my hair or my eyes, my words coming out of a character's mouth. It makes me feel realer to see myself this way, refracted through the prism of his attention.

He is fascinated by my essay writing. Sometimes he will suggest topics for me, like when I go out on three consecutive dates with a man who displays absolutely no personality, just because I know he used to date a woman I think is very interesting. *You should write about all the ways straight guys get vouched for,* he says. *All the reasons people give them a second chance.*

He plays the dating game on his phone too. When my friends see his profile they text me screenshots, ask whether it would be weird to send him a message. I'm always like *Oh yeah oh my god definitely, go for it, absolutely, for sure.*

The first time we have sex it changes everything and nothing at all. It's disorienting to hear the same lines coming out of his mouth that I've heard from other men when everything else about him seems so different. I feel vulnerable playing my version of the character in front of him. The stakes feel higher than I'm used to.

For a while it's fun. We order dinner, stay up late, take long walks across the city, trading secrets and flirting. Sometimes he'll slip some of his ADD medication into my pocket and we'll take it together, spend the day vibrating at the same pitch. *Like being a paper plane with a jet engine*, is how he describes the feeling. He has a knack for metaphor. Everything is always something else.

His job pays him extra to spend nights on call. People need help with their mysterious systems at all times of night and day, and he still has student loans to pay off. The purr of his work phone wakes us both up. I stay quiet as he tiptoes across to the other side of the room and space-bars his computer awake. He speaks to these night clients in a voice wholly unfamiliar to me, smooth as polished glass, cleared of midnight and of any semblance of personality. His face ghostly in the glow of his two monitors.

When he gets me to shut up for the first time, we're in a restaurant. I laugh loudly at something and the sound comes out of him reflexively, a hiss. There's real contempt in it.

Did you just . . . shush me? I ask. I am genuinely confused.

You're so loud, he says. *And you know being looked at embarrasses me.*

I *do* know this. The young writer has endured a series of traumas and hardships over the course of his life that make many ordinary things difficult for him to bear. He has told me so many times, in so many different ways, about his sensitivities, and their origins, and the shame they make him feel. I am supposed to understand that his request is not cruel, but an expression of trust that demands reciprocation: he feels comfortable enough with me to ask me to be quiet, and if I care about him, I'll do it. I'm supposed to be his best friend, the only one who understands him. I want to help. I promise to be quiet. This is the beginning of the end.

One night, after we fuck, I tell him I liked it when he pulled my hair. *Of course you did,* he says, not kindly. *You're a product of your generation.* After a long pause, he adds: *And so am I, I guess.*

Once we're asleep, he gets a call. When he comes back to bed, I roll over to study him through the late-night half-dark. His hands, the bruises on his biceps from my grip, or working out, or both. *You're my natural predator,* I say, sleepily, touching his arm. *Like, in the wild.*

His muscles flex and harden. He pushes my hand away and stares into my eyes. His gaze is hard and unfamiliar. I feel like a pet who's brought a bloodied animal carcass into his bed. *Don't say that,* he says, clipped. My nerve endings blaze with shame or something else.

The next morning, we go out for breakfast and at the end of the meal he pays, like always, before I even get a chance to try.

When we stop having sex his cruelty gets more acute. When we stop talking I feel like I've dodged out of the path of a speeding car. *It's over*, I think. I really think it is.

After a few months of radio silence, we're both invited to the awards ceremony for a writing prize as guests of the same organization. Neither of us wants to go alone. We arrange a temporary truce.

The ceremony is known for its lavish meals and open bar. It's funded by a patron of the arts who weathered a minor scandal a few years ago, after a journalist reported that his wealth involved a multimillion-dollar deal to produce industrial parts for a country with a bone-chilling human rights record. After the story made the rounds, the patron divested himself of the deal and the controversy evaporated. Some people vowed to boycott the awards forever. But the general opinion among most of the artists I talk to is that whenever you trace any significant amount of money back to its origins, you're going to find something unpleasant. Most people still go to the dinner when they're invited, a fact I am able to observe because I do too.

At the entrance to the ceremony, the wealthy patron stands at the front door with his wife, looking each guest in the eye and shaking their hand: *thank you, thank you, thank you.* Inside, the younger writers mill around scoping each other's outfits, while the wealthier elders sit together. The seating arrangements are made in advance, by the organizers; the young writer and I are placed next to each other.

You don't need to know what happens when we stumble out of the party together at the end of the night, drunk off free wine and arguing about who is at fault for the decay of our relationship. If one thing happens to two people at the same time, and each of them leaves with a different story, is it possible for both of their versions to be true?

It doesn't matter. It is not rape. It is not sex. It is not wanted. It hurts but leaves no marks. If you were watching you might wince but not feel forced to turn away. It doesn't matter. I am standing on a dark empty street in the middle of the night, far from home, with a man who is very drunk and very angry with me, and his mouth is on me, and so are his hands, and I can barely move my limbs, and I have been here before; my body knows this moment as a prelude to something darker. Harder to escape.

All at once time threads into itself, forms a clean loop. Suddenly I am ejected from my body, watching myself from the outside, and for a second the familiarity of this experience floods me not with fear or anger but relief. It's been years since the last time a man removed me from myself, and since then I've returned to the memory of this feeling again and again and again. In writing and speaking and dreams, in lawyers' and therapists' and doctors' offices, with strangers and partners and friends or in front of a room full of strangers, I have told and retold it from every possible angle: as explanation, apology, example, defense, assertion, plea, until finally I had told it so many times that all I could feel anymore was the telling. There have been so many moments—holding my breath in front of a screen, flinching from other bodies in a crowd, disappearing under a strange man's gaze or tensing at his touch—when I have wondered whether what happened to me that night, or on all the others like it, could have possibly been *that* bad. Whether I ever really felt the way I think I did.

But in this moment, outside the party with the writer, the distance between past and present collapses and I am joined with myself, in all the times I have been here before. The feeling that links us is seared somewhere deeper than pure memory. We know the things I remember are real because they happened, are happening still, may never stop. Together we stand outside her, witnessing, and wait to be returned.

"Your brain is locked in a vault of silence and darkness inside your skull," the speaker explains. "But it's really good at taking in these signals and extracting patterns and assigning meaning. It takes this inner cosmos and puts together a story of this, your subjective world."

I get a grant from the government to work on my new poems. They direct deposit the money, so I never even touch a piece of paper—the number in my bank account just jumps up. It is more money than I have ever had in my life. I use my benefits from the speaker's agency to buy an IUD and six months' worth of antidepressants, and then I give my two weeks' notice. On my last day, while I'm clearing out my desk, my manager comes by to shake my hand. *Hopefully this will be the last day job you ever have*, he says. It's a very kind thing to say.

FIVE

My two best friends are natural performers. Recently, Deragh was cast as the protagonist in a movie about a troubled young woman navigating the relationships in her life as she goes through a rapidly accelerating emotional breakdown. When the director asked if she thought she knew anyone who could play her best friend, she thought immediately of Doro.

The movie has no actual script. Instead, the two of them build their characters' personalities with the help of the director, and then he puts them in a range of different situations, where they try to do what they think the people they're playing would do.

They've been filming this movie for over a year. The director keeps thinking of new situations. Deragh and Doro ride in the back of a limousine, go skydiving, go to a wedding, tightrope-walk along the guard rail of a terrifying bridge at night. Neither of them is allowed to get a haircut or tattoo that might interfere with their continuity. Most of their scenes will never make it into the final cut.

One day, they were filming a scene where their characters are driving in a car together, having a difficult conversation—Doro at the wheel, Deragh in the passenger seat. The director had told them that Deragh's character was supposed to feel a panic attack coming on as their conversation progressed. She was playing it well. The longer she and Doro talked, the brighter the flush that crept up her throat seemed to glow, the whiter her knuckles as she gripped the seat. She was maybe even shaking a little. Doro was impressed, and a little freaked out.

It wasn't until Deragh started to cry that both of them realized they couldn't tell whether she was still acting. Deragh could sense the pressure sitting on her chest, her breath speeding up past the point where she could reel it back in. Doro was scared, watching her, but the director was silent and the crew kept rolling and the car kept moving. They would probably stop if something was really wrong, she thought. So when Deragh undid her seat belt, opened the door and rolled out of the moving car onto the pavement, Doro yelled out her character's name, not her best friend's. She didn't want to ruin the shot.

Now that I'm a full-time poet, most of my life is about walking around and contemplating things. In the mornings I stroll through the city's biggest park, looking at the patterns the sunlight makes against the ground. The park is full of beautiful dogs whose fur catches the light. I contemplate each one of them, conclude each one is good. At dusk I circle my neighbourhood, looking into the lit windows of its fanciest houses. The light fixtures that hang over their dining room tables look like gym equipment from the future, or mobiles from the '60s, or UFOs drawn by children.

Once a week, I take a two-hour walk to the east side of the city to visit the botanical gardens. I smoke half a joint outside the glass-jewel building and then wander through it from one end to the other, rereading all the plaques I've read before— *cloud forests, plants as medicine*. Sometimes I walk back and forth across the tropical area imagining that I am talking to a reporter, telling them about how important this place was to me while I was working on my latest book.

When I'm done walking, I settle on the bench in the succulent zone and eavesdrop on the families and couples that walk by, jotting down notes on their dialogue. The gardens turn everyone goofy, tender-hearted. People are always pointing to the plants and calling them "this guy." I stay until closing time, when the low angle of the sun turns all the leaves semi-transparent. When I walk back out into the grey, dark, solid slushy city, I feel like I am travelling between worlds.

After a few weeks of not using my mind to make money, my thoughts take on an unprecedented depth and colour. I am experiencing a kind of being alive that almost no one ever gets to, and that fact hovers around me, moves with me when I move. My body is a machine whose primary function is to generate tiny, crucial revelations. Time passes through me without consequence. I'm always noticing my breath.

I start wearing a fanny pack so I can always have everything I need with me at all times: contact lens solution, six pens, a travel deck of tarot cards. I eat nothing but breakfast for two weeks straight. When I find a song I like I listen to it over and over and over again until it is pulverized by the sheer force of my attention. Gravity weakens its hold on me. Whatever I am doing becomes real in its own order. I'm making art for a living, nothing else. This part lasts about three months.

My neighbour is a white weed dealer with long dreadlocks. I learn the forecast from him every morning before I've even opened my eyes; when the sun's out, he goes onto his balcony with a pair of bongos to drum out a greeting to the day.

He, too, works primarily from home. Sometimes I run into him while I'm taking out the garbage, or going to the store. He is almost always shirtless, regardless of the temperature, and holding two phones. One afternoon he comes out to say hello as I am trying to wrench the lid of the compost bin open. *Beautiful day, right?* he says, gesturing at the blue sky. *Really makes you realize all that global warming stuff is bullshit.*

We chat for a while, and he asks whether I have ever heard about the time he tried to convert a school bus to run on vegetable oil instead of gas. I have not.

That was back when I was trying to live without money, he says.

Oh yeah? I ask. *How did that work out?*

Not as good as you might think.

One afternoon I go out to the corner store to buy milk and forget to close the window before I leave. When I return, there is an enormous black squirrel sitting in the middle of our kitchen, chewing on something. An entire bag of the fancy peanut butter granola I bought at the organic grocery store is sprayed across the floor around him. A flash of panic ignites in my chest. *HEY!* I yell. *That cost $8.50!* The squirrel looks up at me, keeps chewing.

In the fall I buy a bus ticket to New York. A few friends who used to be writers in my city are now writers there, and I want to see what their lives are like. Plus the days are getting shorter, my grant is almost gone, my book is not finished, and I'm depressed. I keep returning to the dream of the city of serious artists.

The bus leaves at 6:00 a.m. and is scheduled to arrive exactly twelve hours later. I don't have a return ticket—I'm supposed to drive back in a couple of weeks with some friends, but the plan is still loose, unformed. I don't yet know that this is a bad idea.

The bus takes an hour and a half to get to the border. When the doors open, I'm the first one off; the faster I get through customs, I figure, the faster I can get back on and get to sleep. The rest of the passengers line up behind me. I put my luggage on the conveyor belt and step toward the border guards. Everyone is bored, cold, waiting for their turn, watching me, listening.

The guard asks what I do for a living, and I say I'm a writer.

What kind of writer? he asks.

I write essays. And poems. I'm actually writing a book right now.

He raises his eyebrows. *For a living?* he asks.

I am wearing brand-new sweatpants, no underwear or bra, and an enormous T-shirt, which is so old and worn it's basically just a delicate lattice of tiny holes. It is the outfit I wear while I'm working: at home at night or in the morning while I stare at my computer, typing and deleting and retyping the same few sentences over and over. I am acutely aware of my outfit as the officer asks me more questions about my job. He wants to know how I get paid, whether anyone buys my books, why I do not have a copy of my lease with me or a single boss he can call to verify my claims.

I think about how best to explain that I did have a lease until last month, when our landlord sold our house to a millionaire who wants to tear the building down, and now my stuff is in storage and I'm sleeping in my mother's guest room while Layne and I wait another month to move into an apartment a tenth the size for twice the rent, and that I quit my last day job in a fog of optimism when I got a grant to write a book of prose poems about the rich texture of my own inner life, and now that money is running out and I am still, like a true chump, working on a book that no one will ever read even though it feels like my life hangs in the balance of its completion. I am about two words into the part about the landlord when he goes: *So the government gives you money to write a book?*

I nod.

What happens if you don't finish? Do you have to give the money back?

I open my mouth.

What if the book isn't good? he asks, which is not a bad question. A woman two spots behind me in line laughs a tiny bit, tries to disguise it with a sneeze. I tell him I don't know. Someone opens the door and a blast of cold air hits me in the chest, lighting up the parts of my torso that have become sweaty over the course of the exchange.

The seats in the holding room are bolted to the floor. In one corner there is a bald eagle in a Plexiglas case that could either be taxidermied or a sculpture, it seems wrong to stare.

There are two TVs, one on either side of the room, which is a gesture of either cruelty or mercy given that we are not supposed to use our phone or do anything else while we wait to be called. The air is charged; a room full of people who are incredibly nervous and painfully bored at the same time.

The TVs are mounted where the wall meets the ceiling, so you have to crane your neck to watch. The one on the other side of the room is muted, tuned to a 24-hour news channel. The one closer to me is running what seems like a fake news program for children. On this show, two anchors, one male and one female, sit at large, purple desks and read fun facts about puppies and other cute animals directly into the camera.

Around me, families move in and out of the room, going up to speak to border agents and then sitting back down again. People are dismissed and brought in, seemingly at random. Some people move to the counter, are told something through the Plexiglas, and walk back to their families looking solemn; others just sigh, exasperated, or roll their eyes. The air in the room is simultaneously thick and thin, and everything starts to take on a slightly filmy quality, like I'm hallucinating. There are no commercial breaks in the puppy news show, which makes me think it's playing off a DVD, whereas the cable news on the other side of the room is clearly live. The real-life news is muted, but the puppy news plays at full volume. On the silent TV, I see an ad for the Trump campaign, currently in its final push, screaming silently across the screen. There is a black-and-white photo of Hillary Clinton's face, rubber-stamped with the words "LIAR" and "FALSE." *Cats are so good at jumping because when they land, their feet absorb the shock!* the male anchor says, grinning.

After a couple of hours, someone switches the TV from the 24-hour news to a station playing a marathon of the TV show *Pawn Stars*. There are no clocks in the room, but time breaks down neatly into units of *Pawn Stars*. Two episodes in, as I watch a man named Chumlee silently bullying a grey-haired woman into giving him a $10,000 katana for $6,000, it occurs to me that I understand very little about America.

Eventually I am called to the window. A border agent stamps some forms and stares at a screen for a minute before she spells out the plain facts of my life.

Listen, she says. *You don't have a return ticket. You have no real job. You're "between apartments," you have basically no plans, and you don't have any money. We can't let you in like this.* Then she repeats the key points back to me clearly and slowly: *You don't have a real job, you don't have any future plans, and you don't have any money.*

She is not wrong about me. I can provide her with proof that I exist in the present, but not much more. If she reached through the window and tried to touch me, her hand would go all the way through. She takes me behind the counter and into a room where I am fingerprinted and photographed against a wall that shows how tall I am. She calls a cab to take me back to Canada, a few feet away.

A few weeks later, I buy a return ticket on a flight to New York City. I bring all the paperwork. I only spend half an hour in a holding room this time. It is empty except for a family of two parents and a young child, who sit quietly, waiting to be called. When I leave they are still waiting. My flight lands in New York City on the afternoon of November 8, 2016.

Coming in from the airport, I stare at the ads on the subway, trying to assume the look of someone who has stared at these exact same ads a million times before. (Like all Canadians who visit New York sometimes, I am obsessed with making it seem like I visit New York all the time.) Most of the ads are for apps that deliver food to your apartment, or summon someone to clean it for you.

Others are for an app that connects freelancers who need work to people who need small jobs done—logo design, copy-writing. The purpose of the ads is to convince young people to sign up for the app and provide their services. They are close-up, black-and-white headshots of serious-looking millennials; each one looks directly into the camera with determination and gravity, unsmiling. The text beneath them reads: YOU EAT COFFEE FOR LUNCH. SLEEP DEPRIVATION IS YOUR DRUG OF CHOICE. NOTHING LIKE A STEADY PAYCHECK TO CRUSH YOUR SOUL. Years later I will see these ads cited in books and essays by writers who live in New York City, who actually had to look at them every time they used public transit. Clearly, they make an impression.

It makes sense. The ads encapsulate a conception of value that feels at once timeless and acutely contemporary. The text is as flawless as the most classic lines of poetry: the lit-eral meaning and the truth that shimmers underneath it, each visible through the lens of the other. Standing there with my luggage at my feet, staring into the model's purposefully blank eyes, I wonder about the people who wrote that perfect copy. I wonder where the models came from, and what they told them to look like to get them to make those faces. I wonder whether all these people live in New York City, and whether they take the subway. I wonder how I'd pay rent if I lived here.

That night a bunch of us go to my friend Kelli's place to watch the election results. At first the mood is light and chatty, but as the evening wears on, the air in her small apartment stretches taut.

Around midnight I say, *I'm going to get chips. Does anyone have any requests?*

Cyanide, someone says. Nobody laughs. Outside, the streets are empty, entirely silent.

A week later my friend Haley and I go to see the retrospective of Agnes Martin's paintings at the Guggenheim. The show is hung in order along a large spiral staircase, so that as you move from the bottom of the gallery to the top you progress through the different phases of her career, from her earliest days to the last paintings of her life. It is nice to see someone's entire body of work like this, to move through their life in a spiral, one piece at a time.

About halfway through the exhibit, there's a glass case full of artifacts: a photo of Martin standing in front of the house she built for herself in New Mexico after she left New York, a handwritten piece titled "Advice to Young Woman Artists," a personal inventory of all the places she ever lived, and another of all the day jobs she ever worked. There are thirty-five jobs on the list. I read:

I have worked:

1. as a play ground Director
2. as a tennis coach
3. started two successful businesses
4. on a farm—milking
5. three times at the wheat harvest
6. managed cherry pickers
7. for a mining co. managed Indians horse packing supplies
8. taught three years in country schools
9. as a cashier
10. in a factory
11. in a hamburger stand
12. as a receptionist
13. in a butcher shop

before I'm shuffled off to the side by an encroaching family who wants to see. When I get to the end of the ramp, I start walking back to find Haley. As I pass the glass case again, I notice that the crowd of people waiting to read the list is larger than the group in front of any single painting.

By the time I come home I'm out of money. I apply for jobs and get no responses for weeks, even though the cover letters I send are not bad. I wonder if the people reading them can sense the true meaning hidden under the text: that being a poet has spoiled me for work. Maybe when I say: *On time, curious, eager to learn, prior experience, Microsoft,* they read: *Right now my days are simple. I wash the dishes, I call my mother, and the rest of the time I untangle this knot at the centre of the world. I am a detective in a movie and the mystery is why sometimes when a man touches my bare arm a wave of anger rushes through me so powerfully that all I can do is grit my teeth until I am swallowing a mouthful of sparks. I am trying to know what it means to live in a body with a brain attached, a life that tethers me to the lives of others. Is this not job enough? Must I also become the receptionist at your physiotherapy office?*

When I finally do pick up an interview, it is for the position of cashier at a very large bong store. I spend three hours trying to pick out an outfit that says *I am chill enough to work here but professional enough to take seriously the responsibility of bong salesmanship.* I end up landing on jeans and a Black Flag T-shirt.

The air in the bong store is so thick that the clothes feel incorrect on my body the second I open the door. The smell is a harsh mix of incense and bleach, with bottom notes of something queasier. Not quite the smell of weed, but of weed-related merchandise off-gassing. I can sense it settling into my hair.

The store is enormous. There are racks of novelty T-shirts and drug rugs, counters containing every possible size and permutation of grinder and pipe. There are one million different items you could hide weed inside: fake pens, fake highlighters, fake hairbrushes, fake tools. The walls shimmer with black-light posters. The air is cut with UV that makes my right eye flicker in my skull.

Mostly, though, there are bongs. Bongs in every possible shape, size, colour, material, permutation; ceramic bongs, glass bongs, acrylic bongs; bongs that are sunflowers, bongs that are guns, milk cartons, devils, UFOs, toadstools, Smurfs, Barts Simpson. The longer I stare at the wall of bongs, the more astounded I am by the sheer variation. Crystal formations, lab equipment, flags, all kinds of food. It is, I think, kind of comforting that there is no concept too abstract, no object too complex or unwieldy in its construction, that you cannot find a way to smoke weed out of it.

I tell the guy behind the counter I'm here for an interview and he nods, doesn't say anything or direct me anywhere. Trying not to breathe with my mouth open, I loiter near the front, touching a rack of green T-shirts that just say WEED and attempting to look employable. Eventually, the manager appears.

He takes me down into the basement, which is bright and full of growing supplies—enormous bags of soil, cartoonishly oversized coils of thick green garden hose. In the compressed space of the basement, the grow lights give him a strong aura. He asks me how much I can lift, and what music I'm into. I tell him I'm decently strong and *rap, plus anything I can take a nap to*, which seems like a great answer until it leaves my mouth. He makes some notes on a clipboard, then takes a long look at me.

Ninety percent of this job is telling teenagers we don't sell fake IDs, he says. *Can you do that?* No way, man, I think. *Of course!* I say. *Absolutely. For sure.*

We'll call you, he says, and never does, of course.

A few weeks later I get a message from a friend's ex-boyfriend. He works at a closed-captioning company and has heard that I need a job. He says his workplace is looking for new hires. He suggests I send my resume to his bosses.

Minutes after I do, a call blinks up on my phone. It's the manager of the closed-captioning company. *Do you have a minute?* he asks. *This shouldn't take very long.* His voice is steady, almost painfully sincere, a good boss voice. Reassuring. *Okay*, he says, *so I guess we should start at the beginning.*

It turns out he means not the beginning of the job description or my personal resume, but of the entire closed-captioning industry, which itself begins with the invention of the television. It is immediately clear that the caption boss takes his job very seriously. In a steady monotone, he delivers a well-rehearsed monologue on the history of accessibility in media, CRTC regulations, and the formation of his company, which was recently hired by a prestigious broadcaster in Australia to caption most of their daytime TV.

Five or six minutes into this speech, I realize I have to pee very, very badly, but there's never an opening long enough for me to interrupt. I move into the bathroom and improvise a system where I mute the phone, pee for three seconds, Kegel, mash unmute, deliver a murmur of engagement to indicate that I'm still there, then mute my phone again and pick up where I left off. It takes me over a minute to do maybe ten seconds of peeing this way, but the caption guy does not notice at all. His speech is swelling to a crescendo. The industry exists, he says, to *help* people; to bring ease and comfort into their lives, to bring everyone closer to the world and the world closer to everyone.

There is real emotion in his voice. I feel bad for peeing, but not bad enough to stop.

At the end of his sermon, he pauses. *That all sounds really great*, I say, but he cuts me off. There's one more thing. *We don't have any room on the day shift right now.* A long, significant beat. *Do you think you could work at night?*

Why does a closed-captioning office have a night shift? Does it matter? I'll find out eventually, but at this point I have been buying groceries with my credit card for a month and a half, and the late shift and the day shift pay the same. *Day, night, I'm easy, whatever*, I say, laughing very casually. *Great*, he says, clearly relieved. I wonder for a second what would have happened if I'd said no.

I still have to come in for an official interview. The office is downtown, tucked away on a side street in a sprawling neighbourhood of condos and clubs. The building is almost parodically nondescript, like a film set; all traces of character seem to have been surgically removed from the space. The only concession to decoration is the cactus in the lobby by the elevators—lonely, ancient, browning at the base, rock-solid. It looks like it has been keeping watch over this space for a thousand years.

I arrive early. There's no reception desk, so I sit down on an overstuffed leather chair in the front hallway. From this angle I can see into the main office: a room full of people bent over keyboards, eyes focused on their screens. I try to catch a glimpse of the work they're doing, but from here I can't make anything out. Their typing saturates the air. It sounds like heavy rain on a thin metal roof. Absolutely no one is talking.

The interview is brief. The caption guy says he likes that I'm a writer and that the job is mine if I want it. As he's walking me to the door, he smiles. *You'll be working directly with all these TV scripts, seeing them from the inside out. Maybe this job will help you with your writing!*

For sure! I say, nodding so vigorously I can hear the tendons crunching in my neck.

I learned to type in the mid-'90s, on the very first computer we ever had, a squat grey classic Macintosh my mother inherited from my grandparents that crashed if you looked at it the wrong way. The typing program came preloaded onto the computer. The lessons were boring, but hidden inside of the program was a game designed to test your skills after you'd completed all the levels of instruction. It was the closest thing we had to a computer game, and I played it frantically, aware that at any time my mother would come into the office and tell me to turn off the computer and go outside.

In the game, you're driving alone through the Montana Badlands in a beautiful sports car on a completely empty highway. The landscape around you is drawn from the same colour palette as the jazzy smear you see sometimes on paper cups: rich purple, infinite turquoise, deep, blunt blue. These colours are elemental, the material from which the whole earth is worked. Before you, a range of mountains cuts a jagged line into the horizon, an EKG of the living world. Your car is exactly the same colour as the sky. The vast expanse of desert sand that describes the road around you is pixelated, pointillist, alternating dots of red and blue that vibrate sympathetically against each other but refuse to resolve into a single shade. In the rear-view mirror, you can see the exact same landscape that unfolds before you disappearing in reverse. It's like being at the centre of a palindrome.

Suddenly, a pack of jets comes screaming through the sky. They move from left to right in a neat line, coming to a stop at the exact right-hand edge of your field of vision, trailing a cloud of vapour. They hover there, impossibly, spaced into a perfect military V, and then the vapour begins to change shape. It's forming letters.

Brazen gazelles quickly examined the forward Jeep. Will the kind judges squelch the five or six brazen nymphs? The major will fix a quiet, cozy nook for the vexed, bad Gypsy. Pairs of lazy, knowing oxen came by, quietly evading the jam.

The words disappear as fast as you can read them. You realize you're no longer alone on the road. In your mirror, you can see a bright red sports car. Like the jets, it seems to hover, like time has stopped itself around it—but it must be moving, because you are, and it keeps pace. The driver's windows are tinted; you can't make them out.

The point of the game is perfect synchronization. If you get it right enough, there's a moment when you and the words you're transcribing dissolve so completely into each other that the border between you and the task disappears. No difference between you and what you're typing, a perfect exchange. If you can learn to ride this moment you win, and winning gives you the freedom to coast down the beautiful, uncluttered highway, finally free of the demon anxiety that once seemed always to be right over your shoulder, gaining, just about to overtake you. You can hear the roar of your own engine, the wind whistling, the dull rumble of your opponent at your back. Everything keeps moving. It's your job to keep up.

To get to the caption office, I take the streetcar for about an hour, crowded by people coming home from work. I stop downtown, cut down a side street and cross the building's parking lot, trying not to get hit by a car as all the day-shift people peel out. Punch the code into the keypad, enter the lobby, greet the cactus. Press the button for the elevator, wait forever, eventually get fed up and take the stairs. Push through the thick glass door and walk down the narrow hallway, past the drab communal kitchen, which smells like dollar-store dish soap and always seems to be crusted in a thin layer of white packet sugar.

The hallway opens out into a large, sparsely decorated main office. The walls are exposed brick and the floors are a dull shade of white. Long desks are arranged around the perimeter of the space, with computer workstations spaced out evenly across them. No spot belongs specifically to anyone, and the night shift is so understaffed that I have my pick of positions. I can sit under the windows on the east side of the room, which look out at the empty backyards of a nearby block of houses, or the window on the north side, which looks directly into the manager's office.

The lighting in the office is the kind of fluorescent that lets you see three layers down through your own skin. The only decoration on the walls is a guide to the company's in-house rules for spelling and punctuation that's been attached to the wall outside the manager's office with Blu Tack, though the type is so tiny you'd have to put your nose up against the page to read it properly. When a computer is left untouched for longer than five minutes, a corporate screensaver, installed by the company that owns this company, kicks in: the words BE A TEAM PLAYER next to a stock image of a child floating belly-up in a sky-blue pool.

Closed-captioning, as a job, has two distinct parts: transcription and timing in. Transcribing is the easy part—as long as you can hear and type and type the things you hear, you're good to go. Timing in, where you go back through the episode and link your transcribed text up to the show's action as accurately as you can, is tougher. Not hard, exactly, but complicated. There are a million tiny rules and shortcuts to memorize: character limits, text colours, house style, length. For example: A caption can appear onscreen for a maximum of five seconds and a minimum of one, and there must be a .45 second gap between all captions that end with an end-stop; otherwise, they have to flow seamlessly into each other like water. A caption can't always be the same length as a spoken sentence, and text can appear onscreen in one of four different colours, each meant to signify a different speaker. Two speakers whose lines appear one after the other can obviously never be rendered in the same colour, although this quickly becomes an issue in scenes that feature more than four people speaking at once. Captions need to be raised after a commercial break, with a one-second gap before the next block of transcribed text. If there is already text at the bottom of the screen as a part of the program, you need to raise your caption so both are visible.

There are seventy-six pages of rules like this. Mastering them gives me a tidy, funless pleasure, which is good, because working quickly is the only way to make any money. Captioners are paid not by the amount of time they spend working, but by the number of total minutes in each video they caption. A minute of video can have pretty much anything in it—music, birdsong, total silence, a room full of people screaming over each other so loudly you can't make out a single word—but no matter its content, each minute pays the same. Captioners get $3.00 per video minute for shows we have to transcribe from scratch, and $2.75 for those where the network sends along a script for us to copy and paste in, though these are often booby-trapped with homophones and inaccurate phrasing, and can take more work to edit than you'd put in just doing the whole thing from scratch. A captioner should, on average, be able to hit about forty video minutes per day without breaking a sweat.

There are no mandated breaks at the captioning job. If you want to get up from your computer you can, but every minute of captioning means more money, and every single pause means your money is ticking away. Every second your fingers aren't touching a keyboard, every minute your eyes are off the screen, you are losing money. Answering texts, looking at email, staring out the window, going to the bathroom, eating a snack, letting your mind drift backward or forward for even a second—if you add these things up, they cost too much to justify.

By the end of my first week, I'm pretty close to forty video minutes a day. When I stand in the office kitchen, circling my wrists as I wait impatiently for the kettle to boil, the sound is like someone rolling an office chair over a long sheet of bubble wrap, or walking across a forest floor covered in dry twigs.

+ A scientist and a reporter are standing together on a beach. "Will you ever / put these stick insects / back on the island?" the reporter asks. "Once the rat problem / is under control, / definitely," the scientist says, nodding.

+ A woman is sitting on a blue stage in a pool of icy light, telling the story of her mother's death. The phone call, the silent line, her caught breath, her husband, the paramedics. She says that her mother had never once been to the doctor, not once in her whole life; she never / put herself first. This is the revelation, she explains, for which her brand-new skin care line is named.

+ Two men in matching white suits are standing in front of an enormous metal drum. Everything around them is stainless steel or glowing white. One man flicks a switch and the machine roars to life. The men stare into its depths as a thick yellow substance churns inside, up and down. Pointing a white, gloved finger at something off camera, one man yells: "See over there? / That's where the cheese comes out."

The daytime captioners give me a wide berth as I pass them on my way in, like my shift might be contagious. Not many other people work at night. Aside from me there's Night Manager Steve, a rockabilly couple who never make eye contact with me, Darryl and John, and me. Darryl and John are two very charming men in their late forties who look like alternate-universe versions of each other—either John is a stretched-out, loud Darryl, or Darryl is a shy, squat John. Both have thick, stained skin that looks like hand-tooled leather. The main difference between them is the hair. While John's single shock of bright-white is thin and wiry, Darryl's is impossibly thick and lustrous, like the hair of a boy prince from a fairy tale. It flops down gently in front of his eyes when he's at rest.

It's not clear whether Darryl and John know each other outside of the office, but they both bike to work every day, even in the winter, and they always show up at the exact same time. They move in an aura so thick with cigarette smoke you can smell their presence before they come through the front door.

Darryl speaks to his computer as he captions, keeping up a steady, tense monologue about how much he hates whatever show he's watching. His exclamations lilt like a melody over the steady beat of everyone's typing. *Fuck*, he sighs, sinking deeper into his chair, an episode of British *Antiques Roadshow* humming in front of him. *It's decoupage! Of course. Shit.* John is about a foot taller than Darryl; his girlfriend is a teacher, and they're both into grindhouse movies from the '70s and rescuing cats. His voice sounds like sandpaper scraping across gravel and his default setting is jubilance. *I got five episodes of* Dr. Phil *this week*, he tells me in the kitchen one evening, grinning as he carefully unwraps an individually packaged tea bag. *Can you believe it? That show is monstrous.* He chuckles, shakes his head, stirs his tea, smiling.

Night Manager Steve is shaped like an upside-down mop— floppy hair and stick-thin body—eats an entire large Domino's pizza in his office every shift, never makes eye contact with me or anyone, and leaves his half-empty cans of Red Bull in the fridge for days on end, where their sickly sweet smell seeps into everyone's food.

Some evenings, I will go up to his desk to ask for a new assignment, and as the question escapes my throat I'll realize it's the first time I've spoken to another human being all day. When I speak, a strange queasy sensation moves through me—a pressure bound up with its own release, like the feeling of standing up after your leg's fallen asleep. For months after I leave this job, it will be reflexively triggered in me by the smell of a fresh Domino's pizza.

We mostly caption syndicated American panel shows and Australian daytime TV. It's still not clear to me why an Australian broadcaster has hired a Canadian company to do all their captioning, or how they assign us our work. Some programs come back every week, while others show up once and then disappear completely. Sometimes a hundred episodes of a televangelist's program will descend upon the office like a collective fever dream. You can spend weeks working on just one show, developing a complex, fraught relationship with the quirks in its format, learning its shape the way you'd learn a lover's body—and then you never see it again.

I caption home-renovation shows and an educational program for third-graders about careers in science. I caption Australian *Family Feud* and *MasterChef Australia* and a true crime show that tracks the grisly murder of a beautiful young woman in such detail that I have to periodically step out of the room to scream into my backpack. I caption soap operas and infomercials for revolutionary sprinkler systems and an award show for innovations in contemporary design and a show called *Gardening Australia* about gardening in Australia and a show about a crocodile who loves guacamole called *Crocamole*.

Some shows are fun to watch but bad to caption, like *Antiques Roadshow* (too much text on the screen, too many proper nouns to spellcheck), while others are easy but so boring they make my brain feel liquid, like the grim six-part documentary about the impact of erosion on vulnerable parts of the British Isles. *Judge Judy* is a gift from heaven—fun to watch, so staged it seems morally harmless, and also she's always getting people to shut up so she can monologue, which makes transcribing a breeze. *Neighbours*, the Australian soap opera, provides maybe the best blend of pleasure and ease—it's engaging, endlessly dramatic, with lots of long, silent pauses for significant eye contact. An all-*Neighbours* day is a jackpot. I can polish off five episodes in six hours and leave the office early, richer, and psychically no worse for wear.

The worst, by far, is a program called *The Doctors*. *The Doctors* is a panel show produced by Dr. Phil's son, in which a former Bachelor from *The Bachelor* and a ghoulish plastic surgeon conduct discussions on a range of subjects very loosely adjacent to the topic of medicine. The two men are often joined by a third panellist, usually a hot female psychologist or a hot female sexual health educator or a hot female dermatologist— to offer a hot female perspective. The Bachelor steers the conversation, and his co-host makes inappropriate jokes, laughing like a freshly roused corpse squeezing centuries' worth of dust from his lungs. The hot extra doctor waits patiently for her turn.

The sight of a new *Doctors* on my desktop sets my stomach churning. Every single thing about the show seems haunted: the scrubs the Bachelor wears to host each episode, the howling, disembodied audience, the jagged, violent quick cuts, the blunt blue of the set—debt blue, bus blue, blue like the chairs in a hospital waiting room. The show's content is scaffolded by a logic I recognize from advertising chumboxes on the internet: something shocking next to something gross, something sexual next to something deeply tragic, something disturbing next to something pitiful. Everything in the show's introductory voice-over is either HORRIFYING, LIGHT-HEARTED, or A QUESTION???!?!?: *NEXT, The Doctors surprise A HOME-LESS VETERAN living on FOOD STAMPS with the MAKEOVER OF A LIFETIME!!! THEN, a man marries his pet . . . snake?!????*

A BETTER way to BUST YOUR BELLY FAT!!!! Could your smartphone be KILLING YOU????

Worst of all, the show is a nightmare to caption, filled with graphics and text that appear at random points all over the screen. People talk over each other constantly, and the audience roars so loudly I have to listen to three-second segments a hundred times just to get them right:

WOULD YOU PAY TO SEE A VASECTOMY IN
   REAL TIME?
MEET THE PSYCHO NURSE WHO CYBERSTALKED
   A PATIENT?
COMING UP NEXT, A DOG THAT CAN READ?

These phrases are burned so aggressively into my mind that, after a long day of listening to them over and over, I feel certain they'll last longer in my brain than anything else—like plastic in a landfill, refusing to degrade.

+ In an office building downtown, a man named Ridge is staring at a scale model of a skyscraper. He is in love with the building, or with the model, or what it represents. It has a name. He whispers it into one of the tiny windows while caressing it, gazing into their shiny plastic surfaces, wide-eyed, unblinking.

+ The category is "THINGS THAT GIVE YOU A HEADACHE." The contestant frowns for a second. "Your partner? Your spouse?" The buzzer sounds, and the audience shouts the correct answer all together: "YOUR WIFE!"

+ A woman stands over a spotless gas stove in an immaculate white kitchen, calmly flipping a steak in a cast-iron grill. After thirty or forty seconds, she looks directly into the camera. "Right now / we're just / letting the meat talk."

Every night around 10:00 p.m., Night Steve walks from the kitchen to his office carrying a cup of extremely hot tea filled right to the brim. He holds the cup as delicately as if it were a tiny kitten, walking with what seems like intense focus on every single one of his limbs at once. He moves like a man for whom a large quantity of acid has just kicked in. He looks like someone has slowed his playback to quarter-speed.

One night, about an hour after this ritual, a phone in the main office starts ringing. This never happens, so everyone is lightly startled—except Night Steve, who is so heavily startled there's a *CRASH* from his office that sounds like ten bookshelves plus a storage cabinet full of porcelain figurines all falling over at once. A few seconds later he appears in the doorway, tripping over his own feet multiple times on his way to grab the phone. He gets to it in the last half-second before it stops ringing. It is like watching a man cross the finish line of an ultramarathon.

Hello? he pants into the receiver. Long silence. He pulls the phone away from his ear and shakes it. *Hello? HELLO?????*

After an endless pause, he hangs up. Stares at the phone for maybe thirty seconds.

That was weird, he says.

Everyone just keeps typing.

A caption is a small map of the mind of the person who wrote it. In her misspellings you can see which nouns she'd never heard before, or the direction her mind travels when she mishears a word. In her elisions, you see which words she thinks are necessary to keep, which parts of the idea she thought could be erased without consequence.

Our house style guide says that when a captioner is describing a sound, her language has to be accurate, understandable, and as objective as possible. Draining your writing of all opinion is key. What is the least emotional way to convey that someone is raising their voice, or that something is difficult to hear? How do you describe a distant sound without bringing attention to yourself as listener?

One night, I burn a whole shift on a single forty-five-minute stand-up comedy special. A guy in it has this extended bit where he impersonates the keyboard player from the Bon Jovi song "It's My Life." The joke is that he plays a few notes during the verses, but has nothing at all to do during the big bombastic chorus because there's no keyboard. He never speaks once. The joke rests on the seamless synchronization of his gestures and the music playing over them; it only makes sense if you can tell what's happening. How do you transcribe the absence of something not just accurately, but hilariously, while remaining entirely objective? This problem costs me approximately sixty dollars to figure out.

The Doctors does this thing at the end of every episode called the Word of the Day. Each show ends with the Bachelor delivering a closing monologue about an issue they've discussed on the show—but when he says a certain word, a piercing siren goes off, balloons drop from the ceiling, and the word flashes up on every screen in the studio. *That's our word of the day!* the plastic surgeon yells. Everyone in the audience gets a prize. It is absolutely terrifying, every time.

I start jotting down the words of the day on a small piece of paper next to my computer. At the end of a seven-*Doctors* week, the list reads:

healthy
person
lucky
perception
judge
protect
legal

and then I'm so creeped out I have to stop.

Sometimes, like maybe once every ten videos, a horrible squealing crash will shudder through my headphones. I have no idea what causes the noise, but it makes me feel like I have stuck a wet fork in an electrical socket, like a screaming ghost is gnawing on the inside of my skull. It travels all the way down my spine into the joints of my toes. Every time it happens, I whip my headphones off and slam them down on the desk. No one looks at me or asks what's wrong. If anyone else ever hears the screeching, they never talk about it. Too expensive.

+ The panel is discussing birth defects. Behind them, an enormous screen blazes with the words: BIRTH DEFECTS? Their guest stares directly into the eyes of the host, unblinking, hyper-serious. "Chimerism / is a very rare condition. / Basically, it means / I am my own twin."

+ The panel is discussing a news story about a woman who was murdered in a hotel room. Her killer wrapped her body up in garbage bags and shoved it under the bed, where it lay undiscovered until someone finally complained to the management about the smell in the room. "Crazy!" says the woman with the very shiny hair. "I've stayed in a lot of bad hotels in my time," says the surgeon, "but [indistinct]."

On an average night, the office has one of the most gorgeous soundscapes I've ever heard in my life. The captioning keyboards are deep and sonorous—not like the crisp, nervous clatter of the laptop keys I'm used to. Some captioners type more dramatically than others. John has a light touch, but Darryl sounds like he is slapping the keyboard with the full force of his upper body. You can see his shoulders working through his T-shirt. Night Steve clicks more frantically than he types; you can hear him slamming his mouse all the way from the kitchen.

In addition to closed-captioning, the company specializes in something called "re-speaking," where one person sits in a soundproof room watching a slowed-down episode of a show and clearly repeating every single word of it into a microphone that's hooked up to a computer. Their speech is run through a voice-capture program that transcribes the spoken text so it can be cleaned up and used as a caption. The re-speaking offices are supposed to be soundproof, but sometimes you can hear murmuring through the walls: a guy reciting the lyrics to Sugar Ray's "Every Morning" clear, crisp, sharp and slow, hitting the Ds super hard. A woman transcribing a *60 Minutes* interview with Donald Trump, forced to play both sides.

The captioning office is not far from the lake, and something about its positioning makes it particularly susceptible to weather. When wind hits the outside wall of the building at an angle it makes this high, wavering, wailing sound that splits and multiplies into a ghostly chord. In these moments, the whole office seems to flicker in and out of some alternate dimension, like the signal in a busted old TV. I waste precious minutes paused over my keyboard, holding my phone up to the window, trying to capture this sound on my phone; years later, the files will stay on the desktop of my computer. *1/8/17 SPOOKY CAPTION PLACE, 6/22/17 CAPTION PLACE HOWLING*, etc.

Most nights I leave the office around 1:00 a.m., when the drunk young men of the neighbourhood are spilling out of one club so they can migrate to another. I wait for the streetcar in the doorway of the Dollarama as they come together around me in drifts, then split apart. I feel like a rock in a river. The young men yell for and at each other, collapse on the side-walk, stumble into waiting cars. Their presence calls a cloud of cologne and perfume and vodka and vomit out over the street. They seem to me like a single organic unit, the wildlife of the city. It is like a baptism to stand among them, let them rinse the eerie quiet of the caption place out of my mind.

Standing in the kitchen, circling my wrists while I wait for the microwave, I can see into one of the houses across the street. This room always attracts my gaze; there are no curtains and it stays lit up all night, no matter how late it is. The walls of the room are lined with full bookshelves. I can see a woman inside, sitting at a desk, bent toward a laptop, her face glowing computer-light inside the lamp-glow of the room. In the window I look like I'm standing next to her, wearing the reflection of both offices.

When I get back to my desk, I write an email to the owner. *Is it at all possible for me to switch to the day shift?* Then I search for the addresses of the editors from the big publishing house, the ones who told me to keep in touch.

+ In the night vision colour scheme the sand is blinding white. The tide is moving out. An enormous turtle is propelling itself across the beach at quarter speed. The researchers watch him for ten or twelve seconds until he hits a rough patch and has to stop. He stands for a minute, wrinkly and bathed in weird moonlight. Soft music twinkles in the background. One of the researchers turns to the camera: "Now we're going to measure / the turtle."

On one of my first daytime shifts, there's a solar eclipse. The manager sends out an office-wide email:

> The eclipse today will begin at 1:10 p.m. and will reach maximum coverage of the sun at 2:32 p.m. The blinds in our office have been lowered in anticipation to block out direct sunlight. The hallway area also features huge windows so if you take a call during this time period you may want to move in the other direction. There seems to be an impression among some that the concept of potential retinal damage stemming from staring at an eclipse is either overblown or perhaps an old tale meant to scare kids. I'd encourage you to google "eclipse" and "retinal damage" if you doubt this for whatever reason.

I am briefly touched by his concern for our ocular health, before it occurs to me that we need healthy retinas to caption.

At lunch, when I step out into the parking lot, the entire staff of another company is clustered around a cereal box with holes punched in it—a contraption that lets you look at the sun without fear. When I look at the ground, there are little crescent-shaped shadows scattered across the parking lot. The eclipse is everywhere—patterning the sidewalk, falling all over the parked cars.

When my new book of poems comes out, the publisher books me a small tour—Toronto, Montreal, Ottawa, New York. When I tell the caption people I'll be gone for a couple of weeks, they say there won't be any work for me when I come back. Just like that, I'm a writer again.

In the spring, I visit an accountant for the first time in my life. He works for a firm that specializes in helping artists do their taxes. When I wait to be called for my appointment, I study the decor around me in the waiting room: a filing cabinet, a bowl of clementines, a mini fridge, a stack of old *New Yorkers*. I feel like I am in elementary school, in trouble, about to see the principal and learn my punishment.

The accountant looks over my mess of papers, then explains to me that the caption company's night shift was actually part of a larger strategy to get away with paying full-time employees like contractors. After a year at that job, I'm in the exact same amount of debt, down to the dollar, that I was when I started—but to the government this time, instead of my credit card company.

The appointment costs a third of my rent for the month. *So you write reviews of poetry books?* the accountant asks as I am pressing my PIN into the keypad of his debit machine. *Isn't that a bit like clubbing baby seals?*

He holds the door open for me. *You should look into public speaking if you want to make more money next year*, he says. *I hear people get paid a lot for doing that.* I thank him for the idea and take four clementines from the bowl on my way out.

SIX

I apply for a residency at the Artist's Centre. I am writing a new book for the large publishing house, and I need time and space to work on it. Before I leave, Deragh and Doro and I go to the movies. We see the latest work by a famous director—the one whose last film I saw on a date with the other copywriter at the speaker's agency.

The film is about a man and a woman who fall in love. He is an artist and she is his muse. In their first interaction you can already see tiny signs of everything they'll come to hate about each other. They flirt, get closer, drift apart, explode in an argument that seems like it might wreck them. But after every fight, the man reaches a moment of clarity; he realizes that her presence in his life makes him a better person. Open to the world. In these moments of pure revelation he chooses to come back to her, to start everything again.

Years from now, a famous musician will speak in an interview about her relationship with the director of this film. They broke up decades ago but their fans still romanticize their relationship, post pictures of them together online. She explains that he was cruel, callous, undermining, that he pushed her out of a moving car. *It's a secret that keeps us connected*, she will say to the reporter. She wants to be free of it.

When she releases her next album, one of the songs will be about watching an abusive ex-partner form a relationship with a new woman. Watching the process unfold from the outside, knowing how it felt. *We're the only ones who know*, she sings. And then: *It makes me feel close to you.*

The program at the residency is different than the one I attended last time. This time I have to pay my own money to be there, and instead of a special studio in the forest, I get to work at a desk in my room. Tuition costs several thousand dollars; I use financial aid, the dregs of a grant and a patchwork of freelance cheques to pay for it.

A week before I leave, a man I knew in university writes a blog post about his time in the creative writing program. I remember this guy perfectly. He was older than me, worked in the English department, wanted to be a real writer. I remember him having affairs with women my age and then calling them crazy, making them cry. He was an extra in some of my most humiliating memories, standing on the periphery, glowering at me over the rim of his glass.

I skim through his post, which is very long. He is specific about the things he saw other men do and vague about the things he might have done himself. He says he has nightmares about women he should have "protected." He says that his new career as a teacher has made him "rediscover" his "morality."

Then comes the part that makes me freeze. He quotes my essay from years ago, the one about my time in the program. He takes a scene I wrote and says he saw it happen. He freezes the image and points at himself in the background, sitting behind one of the real writers, rolling his eyes at me. This was real, he says. He was there.

Some parts of the Centre have been renovated since the last time I came, but not all of them. The hallways are exactly as I remember them: same dull carpet, same beige-yellow walls. I can drink at the same bar, swim in the same pool, eat in the same dining hall against the same glass with the same mountains rising dramatically behind me. But the rooms are different. They've been painted so recently that the second you open the door you can smell it; when you do, the past and present split neatly apart.

The new room is decorated like a pricey Airbnb: white walls, blonde wood, LED task lights, a side table that looks like a varnished tree stump. The bed and the desk both face the window, and the showerhead in the bathroom is one of those pancake-sized ones that just *rains* on you. The mattress feels brand new. My first night on it I sleep easy, solid and dreamless, nine hours without moving. The sheets are soft and cool, the bed is deep, the blackout curtains block out all the light.

The next day, after we've all done the formal introduction and been given the talk about avoiding bears, the writers gather at the bar to drink free sweet white wine and check each other out. Everyone asks everyone else what they are working on: *a book about walking, a book about women, a book about my relationship with my father, a book about my sexual relationship with my high school girlfriend,* etc.

I tell everyone the truth, which is that I'm there to write a book about work. Not about trauma, or pain, or fear, or memory, or trauma, or sexual assault. Not about the feeling of being linked to yourself, or being seen. A book about power and language and value, written on my own terms, without reference to anything that makes me uncomfortable or unsettled or unsure of myself. A book that will amplify the things I want to talk about and quietly make the rest disappear.

I spend my first morning of real work taping up index cards on the wall next to my desk, a trick I learned from my TV job. Each card represents a beat, thematic or emotional, within the story. The cards are colour-coded by timeline and theme. The grid they form is symmetrical and clear. I stare at the colours until my vision glazes over and they blur together.

The window at the end of my bed overlooks the patch of forest where all the studios are hidden. Around mealtimes I can see artists coming and going. When the path is clear of humans, elk take their place, ambling back and forth from the woods. The mountains hang behind them like a painting.

My time in this room is so expensive that every moment I spend staring blankly out the window feels like lighting a hundred-dollar bill on fire. But when I turn back to the keyboard it's not much better. For some reason, all I can think about are the novels I didn't know how to write the last time I was here: the one about the black hole in the basement, and then the one about the sinkhole in the city.

I keep thinking about the only scene I knew how to write. The protagonist gains entry to the pool in the basement of her high school or she visits the sinkhole in the middle of the night. For both of her it's pitch black, darker than dark. She knows that if she takes one wrong step it will swallow her whole. In each scene, she backs up or lies down on the pavement, presses her shoulder blades to the cool tile or the concrete, and she listens. The void pulls sound toward its centre. It is like listening to a radio tuned between stations that is melting and exploding all at once. She can hear conversations between students, teachers, cars rushing on the road outside, all kinds of stray music, heavy static, her lost friend's voice, every pitch for every scene she's ever written—all of it rushing forward, wrapping around.

I still don't understand why I kept coming back to this image. Finding new ways to describe what it might be like to be her, standing next to this darkness, feeling its pull.

Days pass. I walk up the mountain and look down at the land below. I walk into town and look up at the mountains. I eat meals in the dining hall. I nurse beers at the bar. When everyone does the call-and-response, I say *I didn't get very much done today* and change the subject.

One night a poet reads my tarot cards. She says the Centre is built over a vein of rose quartz that runs through the mountain; that it gets into your dreams. A lot of the writers are having trouble sleeping, she says.

I watch a lot of TV. The television in my bedroom is sleek and black and mounted to the wall on a swivelling head that lets you pick the angle. I position mine so I can flop down, tap the remote control, and mainline the images directly into my brain. In the daytime I watch basketball games that have been chopped up into different time frames to fit the programming blocks on the sports channel: *Raptors in 60, Raptors in 30, Raptors in 15, Raptors in 5*. I am amazed at the elasticity of time, how you can cut the same story different ways to make it any size. In the evenings, I watch *Jeopardy!* with the novelist whose room is across the hall from mine. At night I watch reality shows. They flow over me like water; I retain nothing. Sometimes, if it's really late, I turn to channel 001, which plays looping, hour-long static shots of empty fields, or flowers waving slightly in the breeze. I fall asleep with the TV on every night, and when I wake up it's always turned off, though I can never remember doing it.

Sometimes I go to the gym. It is one of the facilities, like the dining hall, that the artists share with visiting business people. You can pick them out by the ferocity of their workouts and the complex, technical nature of their outfits. I try to mimic their focused expressions as I maintain a slow, unchanging pace on the treadmill for exactly thirty minutes.

When I run I always listen to the same song. It is the most popular song in the world, by the most popular rapper on earth, and it is catchy the way only certain kinds of pop songs can be—where the only cure for what they do to you is to listen to them twenty more times in a row. The song is about how the world's most popular rapper achieved his considerable success through the grace and generosity of God, despite the interference of other human beings. How every development in his life has been driven by a force stronger than his mere mortal will.

The song relies on a sample that sounds like someone playing simple chords on a pipe organ. It's a perfect bar of music; shifting up and down behind the rapper's voice, dappled like sun through a gauzy curtain. *Bad things,* he sings in my headphones. *It's a lot of bad things / That they wishin' and wishin' and wishin' and wishin' / They wishin' on me.* I listen to the song on a loop so clean that it's impossible to tell where it begins or ends.

A few days before the program is over, I go to a lecture by one of the mentors, an author who writes about Indigeneity and decolonial love. *Poetry,* he says, *ought to cultivate a curiosity about the end of the world.*

That night, I convince two novelists to go into town with me to the movie theatre. We watch a movie I have already seen, the one I saw with my best friends before I came here. The second viewing is useful. Another layer of meaning reveals itself. I can't tell if I'm noticing things I missed the first time, or whether there are themes inside the story that are impossible to understand until you've seen them more than once.

On my last day at the Centre I go swimming. The ceiling of the aquatic centre is all glass, sloped downward so that snow will slide off it. The day outside is perfectly clear; the pool seems filled with light instead of water.

There's no one else there when I arrive, not even a lifeguard. Still, satellite radio plays over the speakers—a top 40 station, so I can still listen to the famous rapper's song. The room's hollow acoustics make the sound echo and bounce, so the music always seems both a few steps ahead of and behind itself. I lie back and float, looking straight up. The sky, the water and my body are all reflected together in the glass, like they're all parts of the same single image. I stay there like that for a long time, wondering if anything about this will eventually be something I can use.

Acknowledgements

Writing is expensive, and it takes a long time. This book would not exist without support from the Canada Council for the Arts, and I would never have been able to write any of the other books mentioned inside of it without grants and assistance from the Toronto Arts Council, the Ontario Arts Council, the Conseil des arts et des lettres du Québec, and the Banff Centre for Arts and Creativity.

I am grateful to my agent, Martha Webb, for her patience and kindness and rigour, and to Sara Peters for introducing us. Thank you to Craig Pyette for his keen editorial eye and generous readings, and to Anne Collins, Sue Kuruvilla and everyone else at Penguin Random House Canada who helped this book become real.

Thank you to Moira, Brian, Dad, Morwyn, Augie and Sass for conversations that all made their way in here one way or another; to Mike Chaulk and Layne Hinton for gold standard best friendship; to Haley Mlotek for being my mom and also my daughter and also my wife; and to Rudrapriya Rathore, Carlyn Bezic and Yanyi for sharing your time and art and insights with me. To Carlo Spidla, obviously, forever. To my mother, for showing me how to do all of this. And to Deragh and Doro, who wrote it with me. I love you.

EMMA HEALEY has published two collections of poetry, *Begin with the End in Mind* and *Stereoblind*. Her poems and essays have been featured in the *Los Angeles Review of Books*, the *FADER*, the *Hairpin*, *Real Life*, the *National Post*, the *Globe and Mail*, the *Toronto Star*, the *Walrus*, *Canadian Art*, *Raptors HQ* and many other outlets. She was formerly poetry critic at the *Globe and Mail* and a regular contributor to the music blog *Said the Gramophone*.